Walther Ziegler:

Foucault

in 60 Minutes

Translated by
Alexander Reynolds

My thanks go to Rudolf Aichner for his tireless critical editing; Silke Ruthenberg for the fine graphics; Lydia Pointvogl, Eva Amberger, Christiane Hüttner, and Dr. Martin Engler for their excellent work as manuscript readers and sub-editors; Prof. Guntram Knapp, who first inspired me with enthusiasm for philosophy; and Angela Schumitz, who handled in the most professional manner, as chief editorial reader, the production of both the German and the English editions of this series of books.

My special thanks go to my translator

Dr Alexander Reynolds.

Himself a philosopher, he not only translated the original German text into English with great care and precision but also, in passages where this was required in order to ensure clear understanding, supplemented this text with certain formulations adapted specifically to the needs of English-language readers.

We are […] in the panoptic machine, invested by its effects of power, which we bring to ourselves, since we are part of its mechanism.[1]

Bibliographic Information held by the German National Library: The details of the original German edition of this publication are held by the German National Library as part of the German National Bibliography; detailed bibliographical data can be found online at www.dnb.de.

© 2021 Dr Walther Ziegler
1st Edition March 2021
Jacket design and graphic design for the whole book: Silke Ruthenberg, making use of illustrations by:
Raphael Bräsecke, Creactive – Studio for Advertising, Comics & Illustrations
© JackF - Fotolia.com (image-frames)
© Valerie Potapova - Fotolia.com (image-frames)
© Svetlana Gryankina - Fotolia.com (speech-balloons)

Publisher and Printing:
BoD – Books on Demand, Norderstedt
ISBN 9-7837-5342-268-8

Contents

Foucault's Great Discovery

Michel Foucault (1926-1984) is surely the most fascinatingly elusive philosopher of the 20th century. He was often described as one of the greatest of the "Post-Structuralists" but tended, himself, to reject all classifications. His thinking, he claimed, was of a sort that fit into no philosophical school or tradition:

I am an experimenter and not a theoretician.[2]

When tackling a particular topic, he had, unlike other philosophers, no ready-made theory that he could apply again and again:

I never think exactly the same thing (as I did in the previous book) because all my books are, for me, like lived experiences [...]

7

I only write each book because I don't yet know exactly what I think about whatever it is I set out to think and write about [...] I write, indeed, precisely in order to change and in order not to think whatever it was I thought before.[3]

Foucault was, indeed, undoubtedly a thinker who followed his own unique path, as is indicated by the intriguing titles of his books: *Madness and Civilization, Discipline and Punish, The Order of Things, The Use of Pleasure, The Care of the Self.* Very few philosophers brought so many animating and vivifying impulses into the social and cultural discussions of the late 20th century as Foucault did. Although he cannot be said to have founded any school or movement of his own, he very definitely counts among those philosophers whose influence and significance have lived on after their deaths. Indeed, it can even be said that the more time passes since his premature death, the more relevant his philosophy becomes. That this is so is something we should be both pleased and perturbed about. Pleased because Foucault's key idea is one which has definitely survived his death and which continues to be passionately discussed even today; perturbed because this key idea is indeed a worrying, even alarming one:

[...] One can certainly wager that Man would be erased, like a face drawn in sand at the edge of the sea.[4]

Appointed at a very young age to a professorial chair at the Collège de France, perhaps the most eminent of all among the small select number of elite colleges and universities in Paris, Foucault declared this disturbing news of

[...] the end of Man [...].[5]

to auditoriums so full that many could only watch on screens set up outside.

By this thesis of "the end of Man" Foucault did not, indeed, mean, as might at first be supposed, the physical extinction of the human species, for example by an atomic war or global warming. No, for Foucault, to borrow a phrase from the poet Eliot, the "end of Man" arrives "not with a bang but a whimper". Mankind's "death" is not a physical but rather a psychological one. What Foucault is trying to tell us, in other words, is that Man as we have hitherto known him, namely as a free, self-determined being capable of spontaneous pleasure and happiness, is bound to slowly die away and vanish. This being that we have called "Man" will be gradually dissolved away into the structures of what Foucault calls our "carceral", meaning "prison-like", society", in the same way a face drawn in the sand is dissolved by the incoming tide. Each new wave obscures its outlines more and more, until there is nothing left at all.

Foucault's arguments, then, run fundamentally counter to the story that is usually told of how modern Man, from the 18th-century Enlightenment onward, has gained more and more self-confidence and has come to enjoy an ever larger number of individual liberties. Directly contradicting this view, Foucault denies that scientific progress and humanism have made the world we live in century by century an ever better one. The opposite has been the case, he argues. Humanity had set out, indeed, in that Enlightenment era of political emancipation and technical innovation, to free itself, with the help of science and the power of knowing subjectivity, from all constraints of Nature and religion. But mankind's accumulated knowledge had, in the end, brought about precisely the opposite result:

> If the will-to-knowledge is just now attaining its greatest magnitude and breadth [...] it is not thereby providing human beings with a sure and steady dominion over

> Nature. On the contrary [...] it is acting to destroy all protecting illusions; it is annihilating the unity of the human subject and is setting free in us everything that tends to work toward our disintegration.[6]

It already tells us very much that Foucault, when talking about the human impulse to invent and discover, uses this phrase "will-to-knowledge", clearly modelled on Nietzsche's phrase "will-to-power". The phrasing alone indicates that Foucault's, like Nietzsche's, is a dark, power-centred view of modernity: one which holds that, even if this "will-to-knowledge" unleashed by the century of Enlightenment succeeded in producing immense technical progress and freeing Man from medieval illusions and superstitions, it thereby replaced the old irrational structures with new, rational ones which, just because they are founded in reason, tend to put even tighter restrictions on human freedom than religious faith and superstition ever did. Modern science, with its new rational insights, and the humanism that goes hand in hand with it, bring only the appearance of improvement. Because they are not really knowledge but rather a will-to-power that has merely taken the form of a will-to-knowledge, forming a sort of iron straitjacket that seizes and subjects to discipline society as a whole.

Humanity, then, through the unshackling of its own powers of reason, only set itself, without intending to, on a path to its own disintegration. Foucault's books tend, in fact, to extend this pessimistic analysis of the consequences of Enlightenment a little way back beyond the period most often linked to this idea, the 18th century, into the 17th: the so-called "Classic Age" when the political and cultural importance of

Foucault's native France was at its height. These two hundred years are, for Foucault, the decisive time in modern history. It is here that "the abolition of Man" begins. Above all because it is in these centuries that scientists begin to make Man himself an object of scientific research. These centuries see the birth of all the so-called "human sciences", such as biology, psychology, psychiatry and criminology, which produce an entirely new, systematic type of knowledge of what it is to be a human being. For the first time, science provides precise definitions of "normal" and "deviant", "healthy" and "sick", "natural" and "perverse" behaviour. All across Europe there arise institutions designed to remove the "insane" from the midst of the society of "normal people":

In order, then, for the great centres of confinement to be able to arise all over Europe at the end of the 18th century a certain knowledge regarding what was "mad"

and what was "not mad", a certain knowledge regarding order and disorder, had already to lie to hand.[7]

In his doctoral thesis *Madness and Civilization*, with which he attracted great attention already at an early age, Foucault showed that, for several centuries stretching from the Middle Ages through to early modernity, people exhibiting highly deviant behaviour were tolerated and allowed to live with others in the very midst of society. These people were often, indeed, mocked and made fun of, as eccentrics or "village idiots", in the small communities in which they lived. But they were tolerated and accepted none the less. It was only as modernity advanced, in the 17th and 18th centuries, that a great army of scientists and scholars began to swarm around these people, to define their various conditions as forms of "psychopathology", and to concentrate and confine them in "madhouses". From this point on, says Foucault, there begins "the great confinement"[8] of madness. Madness now becomes completely sequestered from reason and defined as a dangerous "unreason". It is only through this determination by science that the madman is definitively stamped as mad:

The madman cannot be mad just for himself but only in the eyes of

some other person, who is alone able to separate the clouding of reason from reason itself.[9]

But this is not all. In the 17th and 18th centuries it is not just psychiatric institutions but gigantic mass prisons that come, on the basis of supposed scientific insights, to be erected for the first time. Punishment and discipline become ubiquitous. Already previous centuries, indeed, had seen dungeons and jails in which criminals, or enemies of local rulers, had been locked away. It had even happened that individual lawbreakers were sometimes displayed in cages or "put in the stocks". But the mass internment of tens of thousands of criminals in prisons and penitentiaries of the sort we know today was, Foucault argues, an achievement of recent centuries.

In what is probably his most-read and best-known work, with the highly significant title *Discipline and Punish*, Foucault describes the introduction of a new, rationalistically-perfected type of prison by the jurist and social philosopher Jeremy Bentham. Bentham sketched out, in 1756, a design for a so-called "panoptic" prison in which all the cells would be concentrically arranged around a single central tower. This meant that the warder would be able to observe, through a narrow slit in his tower, every one of the prisoners, without being in turn observed by any of them:

In the central tower one sees everything without ever being seen.[10]

It is not, indeed, practically possible on this model for the warder to keep all the cells in view at once. But it is enough, as Foucault explains in elucidation of Bentham's intentions, that the prisoners know that they could, in theory, be being observed. This will cause them to behave, off their own bat, as if they are under constant surveillance: self-discipline takes the place of discipline. In modern systems of confinement this constant surveillance, or belief in being constantly surveilled, is aided by a total control of body and mind through a strict regulation of daily tasks and schedules. The ringing of bells and buzzers at regular intervals signals the hour and minute for getting up, working, eating, sleeping or undergoing corporal punishment. And all this takes place with the prisoners gathered together in the same strictly defined "panoptic" space. It is here that Foucault formulates what is probably his best-known and most provocative thesis:

The panoptic schema was destined to spread throughout the social body [...] Its vocation was to become a generalized function.[11]

The prison, then, with its techniques of disciplining and of seeing and being seen, becomes, suggests Foucault, the model and core of our whole civilization. The teacher looks down, from his raised lectern, on the students; the boss, from his office high above the shop floor, on his workers. The system of the panoptic prison thus spreads out into all regions of the social body:

It serves to reform prisoners, but also [...] to instruct schoolchildren, to confine the insane, to supervise workers, to put [...] idlers to work.[12]

At school, in the army barracks, in government offices, in mental institutions, in the workplace and even when drawing unemployment, modern Man is penned into specific locations, has all his data recorded, and is compelled to conform to certain fixed processes. Our modern institutions are, just like Bentham's ideal prison, perfect systems of disciplining that enable us to eliminate any individual who is a source of disturbance and prevent all others from becoming so. Because even those who have not (yet) been shut out of society know that, if their behaviour becomes in any way deviant, they can suffer just this fate at any time. The words that we throw at each other in jest, such as "You're crazy" or "Watch the men in white coats don't come and get you" prove, in this light, to be truer than we think.

The fear, be it conscious or unconscious, of being thrown oneself, as someone abnormal or delinquent, into a mental asylum or house of correction creates, Foucault argues, a permanent pressure to conform. The sense of always being under surveillance that is characteristic of such institutions has come by now to characterize also the daily life of millions of human beings in our modern societies.

This dissolution of the human being and of human freedom in a society of total coercion is, for Foucault, in the last analysis the result of a long process which he exposes and documents like an archaeologist. In what is perhaps his main work, *The Order of Things*, and also in later writings he does indeed describe himself as an archaeologist, inasmuch as he digs out the deeper-lying strata of what passed for knowledge in those eras which form, in the end, the rigid infrastructure of our societies today and thereby determine "the order of things":

By "archaeology" I mean [...] a field of research which looks more or less as follows: the knowledge, the philosophical ideas and the day-to-day opinions of a society, but also its institutions, its business and law-enforcement practices or its morals and customs [...].[13]

Thus every society, our own included, is pervaded, Foucault argues, by a certain implicit "knowledge", which one might also call a governing inner truth, which animates and guides each society's institutions as well as its individuals. For this reason, "truth" and "power" are, for Foucault, not regions of human experience that can ever be separated or isolated from one another.

It is important, I believe, to understand that truth neither stands outside of power nor is itself without power [...] Truth is something of this world. It is in this world, under the effect of many sorts of compulsion and coercion, that it is produced [...].[14]

Truth, in other words, is nothing that is eternally valid but rather something that is produced by each of a long series of different societies. The truth "produced" in Ancient Greece, for example, was a different one from that "produced" in the Middle Ages, or in our own modern democracy. Thus it was believed in Greece, as an incontrovertible fact, that slavery was something entirely natural, so that slaves were an almost self-evident feature of every decent household. Even Plato and Aristotle accepted this as incontrovertible truth. Today, however, we are "producing" another truth. For this reason, Foucault can say:

Every society has its own ordering of truth, its own, as it were, "general politics" of truth.[15]

But this production of truth on the part of each society can be a dangerous and fateful thing. Because this "ordering of truth" that Foucault refers to itself orders and determines all public and private discourse. It establishes what can and cannot be said and even what can and cannot be thought. There is, in Foucault's view, for the individual human being

21

simply no way out of this compelling objective structure. In this respect Foucault really does belong to
that intellectual movement that dominated French
thought in his early years: structuralism. He sees
our entire sense of life and sense of self, right down
to our sexuality and other sensual pleasures, as being profoundly marked and moulded by the social
structure of truth and the "politics of truth" that this
dictates. Thus, our sexuality is no longer any kind
of original or natural need over which we ourselves
have some degree of control but rather the product
of discourses steered by power:

> My main concern will be to locate the
> forms of power, the channels it takes
> [...] in order to reach the most tenuous
> and individual modes of behaviour
> [...], how it penetrates and controls
> everyday pleasure.[16]

It is indeed in his four-volume work, *The History of
Sexuality*[17], that Foucault pursues this question far-
thest. Through what channels does power control our

behaviour? How does it gain access to and mould our sexuality? He invites us to dive down with him into the deepest strata of our social truth-production:

As for me, to my own self I felt like a fish that, far underwater where he could no longer be seen, was following a deeper, more coherent, more rational path.[18]

Foucault chose, in the end, to develop his key idea in three large steps. Firstly, he set about digging and searching, like an archaeologist, to locate and identify those old social convictions, ways of thinking, and institutions which have, over the course of time, produced the moral and scientific attitudes we have today. In a second step he critiqued these forms of knowledge which we have inherited from the past, since they result in many human beings becoming marginalized, cut us all off from our true needs and even cause our very humanity to die away. And in a third and final step he attempts to sketch out how, despite the fact of our being helplessly given over into a coercive, punitive society, we might develop a certain "art of living" which would reconcile us, at least to a small degree, with our deeper needs and our existence as human beings.

What does this "art of living" look like? Is it still possible at all for an individual subject to break out of the society of surveillance and coercion? Is "Man" really dying? Is Foucault right with his famous analogy between modern society and a "panoptic" prison? Do we really all feel ourselves to be under constant controlling observation? Is our present Digital Age the very culmination of this development: the highest possible point of surveillance and self-inflicted punishment? One thing at least is certain: Foucault's ideas are of disturbingly close relevance to the lives we live today.

Foucault's Central Idea

The Archaeology of Knowledge: How We Became What We Are

In the books *The Archaeology of Knowledge* and *The Order of Things* Foucault describes his own philosophical approach in the following terms: the decisive thing is to have no prejudices, either as a philosopher or as a human being. We need, Foucault argues, to recognize the reality of the world in just the way that this reality shows and reveals its own self. This means that we must let what really counted as knowledge in each particular era speak out in its own terms and words. And the best way to achieve this is to unearth and study, as does an historian or an archaeologist, the real, authentic documents, artifacts, artworks and chronicles testifying to the events and institutions of each respective epoch and then to reveal in these documents, artifacts and chronicles the structure common to everything that passed, in every society respectively, for "truth" or "knowledge". Foucault's books stand out, indeed, in containing an enormous variety of such documents and artifacts, ranging from construction plans for prisons and asylums, through historical chronicles to literary works and even, in one well-known passage, to a detailed description of the "quartering" of someone convicted of parricide:

This way of researching interests me for the following reason. It avoids the whole problem of asking: which came first, the theory or the practice that corresponds to it? I deal, in fact, with practices, institutions and

theories all in the same way and on the same level [...] and seek out the form of 'knowing' common to them all that makes them all possible, the stratum of their constitutive historical knowledge.[19]

All previous philosophy, Foucault argues, has paid attention either just to one or just to the other of these two aspects. It has either proceeded idealistically, taking nothing seriously except the element of theory and conceiving of the "knowledge" of an epoch only in terms of the supposedly most important ideas, i.e. the thoughts of kings, philosophers and geniuses. Or it has proceeded purely materialistically, paying attention only to the economic and social conditions existing in each epoch, claiming that it was these that determined everything else. But both these approaches, Foucault goes on, are wrong. The way to proceed is rather to hold solely to the deeper structures of each epoch's notion of "knowledge" and to the institutional "truth-production" that derives from it.

As regards this key position, certainly, Foucault was a "Structuralist" through and through. Thus, he joined his voice to that of several others, already during his student years directly after World War Two, in rejecting Sartre's Existentialist claim, so fashionable and influential at the time, that the life of Man was one of radical freedom and radical individual decisions. On the other hand, however, he came, around the same time, also to reject the opposite claim of Marx and the Marxists whereby the decisions and beliefs of individual subjects are always only the consequences of their economic and social positions:

> We discovered that [...] it was not enough to say sometimes, with one camp, that the individual was radically free and other times, with the other camp, that the individual was fundamentally determined by social forces.[20]

The approach, alternative to both of these, that Foucault eventually chose to adopt was to concentrate solely on the underlying "deep structure" or, as he puts it, "the stratum of constitutive historical knowledge" from which both the actions and ideas of individuals and their economic and social circumstances emerge:

> In short, it is a matter of relieving the individual of his role as an original foundation of everything [...] and of analysing this individual rather as a variable function of discourse.[21]

The individual, then, is, when looked at in terms of Foucault's Structuralist consideration of these questions, no longer the source and origin of his or her own thoughts and actions but rather only a "variable function of discourse". This means that, although we do indeed express our personal opinions as individual subjects, we are able to express them only in ways laid down for us by the functions assigned through the ruling discourse of our age or society. We can only ever say what the limits and restrictions of this ruling discourse makes it possible to say, and no more:

> [...] One is "in the truth" only when one obeys the rules of a kind of discursive "police force" which is automatically set in motion every time one engages in an act of discourse.[22]

When he speaks of "discourse", then, we must understand Foucault to be referring not just to the concrete conversations that go on between individual human beings but also to the interwoven structures of power and knowledge that are always also in play, in each particular society, when any of this society's members engages in such verbal or practical interaction with another member. Foucault ascribes a decisive influence on all we say and do to these pervasive structures:

> I proceed on the assumption that in every society the production of discourse is at the same time monitored, selected, organized and directed into specific channels [...].[23]

This means of course in the end that, according to Foucault, the "freedom of self-expression" that our modern societies talk so much about is nothing but an illusion. Our "free self-expression" is so profoundly marked and pervaded by the imperatives of each society's ruling discursive structures that it is nowhere near so "free" as we flatter ourselves it is. Every contribution an individual makes to any sort of discussion or debate is made within one, or several at a time, of these rigid structures, such as the grammars of our languages, the customs of our countries, our respective political systems or moral codes, our commonly held beliefs, certain dominant styles and methods of education, the senses of the beautiful or the appropriate shared by all. In short, all that we say and do we say and do within the structures of the "constitutive knowledge" of our respective times and places. This "constitutive knowledge" has altered, indeed, in the course of the centuries but at each particular time and place it rigidly determines the character of what Foucault calls "discourse". We may say, then, that the knowledge that is produced by the discourses tightly governed by such structures is not truth *per se* but only that which, in the discourse of each respective epoch, passes for being true:

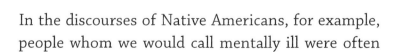

Discourses on mental illness, criminal delinquency or sexuality do not tell us what the individual is. They only tell us what he is within the framework of a specific, extremely particular "truth-game".[24]

In the discourses of Native Americans, for example, people whom we would call mentally ill were often admired or revered. They were believed to have been touched by the god Manitu. In the discourses of the Middle Ages, however, they were looked on as possessed by the Devil and attempts were made to exorcise them. Only in recent centuries has the accepted "discursive truth" become that they suffer from psychopathologies, so that a veritable army of doctors now flock around every such individual to provide him or her with "therapy". For Foucault, however, we do not learn from, or in, any of these three very different discourses what the individuals they focus on really are. We learn in each case only what each respective local or epochal discourse *considers them to be* . In this respect our modern psychiatrists are no different from the members of Native American or medieval Christian societies. In all three cases, the "knowledge" applied is simply a "constituted knowledge" that corresponds in every detail to the various forms of pre-existing "constituting knowledge" that underlies it:

> Discourse is the entirety of the coerced and coercing meanings that pervade our social conditions and circumstances from top to bottom.[25]

Are our individual thoughts and opinions, then, just foam on the surface of the endless ocean of socially coerced and coercing "discourse"? Are we, in Foucault's view, just puppets of the structures of "constitutive knowledge"?

We both are and are not such foam, such puppets. Foucault's thought is a thought which proceeds along a razor's edge between the recognition of this terrible situation and its acceptance. On the one hand, in his work as an "archaeologist of knowledge", he soberly reveals the iron-hard, rigid structures of discourse and knowledge to which we are all, as individuals, helplessly exposed and subjected and which, indeed, mould and form us into the individuals we are. But on the other hand we see him, once this sober and bleak work of revealing these structures has been completed, do something amazing. It turns out that, in describing the structures of our "truth-production" and the dominating, coercing structures of our discourse, in such stark and provocative terms, he achieves the effect of bringing us, his readers, to the realization that we cannot simply passively accept these dominating structures, nor should we want to. Thus, although Foucault is, in a first movement, a pure "descriptivist" who does no more than "tell it just as it is", these very descriptions are such as to prompt us to adopt a critical, resisting attitude to the world "just as it is". The results of Foucault's researches serve to undermine the beliefs we have uncritically adopted, inasmuch as they show what narrow-minded, partial and partisan viewpoints lie at the origin of what we still take to be "truth". Paradoxically, then, it proves to be precisely by recognizing how rigidly determined we are by the structures that have us in their grip that we acquire a chance of achieving a freer thought and thereby possibly a freer action:

There are times in life when the question of knowing if one can think differently than one thinks, and perceive differently than one sees, is absolutely necessary [...].[26]

Acquiring an understanding of how far we are imprisoned in a cage of structural determination enables us, precisely, to rattle and shake the bars of this cage, so that we are no longer compliant and entirely powerless prisoners of the ruling, determining be-

liefs and are in a position at least to transform our
way of thinking about them:

> The "essay" – which should be
> understood as the assay or test by
> which one undergoes changes [...] – is
> the living substance of philosophy [...].[27]

It was this twist that Foucault gave to the Structuralist critique of knowledge, taking it in the direction
of "the attempt to change one's own self", that has
led to him being described rather as a "Post-Structuralist" than as a "Structuralist". His philosophical
project is indeed in the first instance, just like that
of the more classical representatives of French Structuralism, the project of soberly and neutrally describing all the manifold ways in which our knowledge
and action is determined and directed by structures
beyond our control. But the results that Foucault arrives at in his pursuit of this project are so shocking
and provocative that they entirely shatter the limits
of the initially sober and unemotional Structuralist philosophy. That is to say, these results amount
in the end to a brilliant and passionate critique of

the way in which knowledge is produced in contemporary society and in the relentless tendencies to marginalization, exclusion and domination that this "knowledge-production" involves. That Foucault's philosophy identifies and names these tendencies, for the first time, as the repressive and destructive tendencies that they are does not, indeed, amount just in itself to overcoming and removing them. But this identifying and naming does mean the opening of a first revealing tear in the veil that has hitherto provided these tendencies with their legitimacy.

Madness and Civilization – The Excluding Confinement of Unreason

Much of what is essential in Foucault's philosophical project is to be found already in the massive five-hundred-page text which he submitted, when still a young man, as his doctoral thesis: *Madness and Civilization: A History of Insanity in the Age of Reason*. In this text he describes the basic structure of Western "Reason" as a whole by the light specifically of the way Western societies have dealt with madness. He examines here not just the criteria which are used by modern, contemporary science to separate the "mad", or mentally ill, from the "normal" but also the various ways that madness was dealt with in earlier epochs. He reveals, for example, that even as late as the Renaissance society had been "hospitable" to madness and the mad in a way which seems strange to us today. The "crazy" were not simply locked away but were rather accepted and tolerated in their "different way of being":

This world of the early 17th century is strangely hospitable, in all senses, to madness.[28]

We might sum up the gist of Foucault's argument in this long book by saying that, here, he describes the birth of the modern ideal of "Reason" by describing "Reason"'s attempts to demarcate itself from its natural opponent and competitor: the personified "Unreason" of madmen and madwomen. By understanding, Foucault explains, what counted for each respective epoch as "mad", "crazy", "irrational", and how each respective epoch dealt with those who were looked on as "mad", we also come to grasp the deepest and most essential contours of each epoch's "Reason" and of what it meant to think and act "rationally" at that specific time. Madness and how it is related to are, Foucault contends, an infallible indicator of the historical state of Reason, be it as Reason's mirror image or as the sum of all that is split off from Reason and excluded from it:

Being *vis-à-vis* Reason, madness displays a dual nature: it is at the same time *on the other side* from Reason and under *Reason's gaze*.[29]

Madness, in other words, is constituted as both that which is opposed to Reason and that which must remain constantly under Reason's surveillance. This aspect of "constant surveillance" is a decisively important one for Foucault because, as he argues, it is only from that "perspective of the observer" so characteristic of Reason, for example the perspective of "science" and of the "scientist", that the "madman" is "mad" at all:

In the "state of Nature" there is no such thing as madness. Madness comes to exist only with the emergence of society. It does not exist outside of the forms [...] which isolate it or which [...] exclude or confine it.[30]

It is only against the background of a precise definition of what is to count as "reason" that madness can come to be perceived as "unreason":

[...] Madness [...] is total unreason which is perceived against the background of the *structures of the reasonable*.[31]

But this was not always so. In the Middle Ages and in the Renaissance, Foucault points out, madness was not seen as such a "total unreason" that Reason needed to combat and place under a taboo. On the contrary, madness had a presence and a role even in the "best society": kings, princes and high nobility invariably maintained a "fool", to play the role of clown or jester, at their courts. This figure, moreover, enjoyed the special "fool's freedom" of being able to speak out the truth as he saw it, quite regardless of all reason, logic or social etiquette. In the theatre of the time too the figure of the Fool or the Madman, and the madness itself that he personified, exerted a special fascination:

[...] The hallucinations of his madness have more power of attraction for fifteenth-century Man than the [...] reality of the flesh.[32]

We find the proof of this, argues Foucault, in the work of painters such as Stefan Lochner, Matthias Gruenewald, Pieter Bruegel and Hieronymus Bosch. The last of these, for example was admired and honoured above all for his nightmarish and apocalyptic portrayals of scenes and events in Hell. Here, toads are shown squatting on genitalia, while gnomes and monsters with the heads of fishes, birds, pigs or various crueller predatory animals are shown tormenting and even devouring their human victims. Grotesque punishments are shown, such as arrows transfixing the anuses of the tormented souls. These phantasms, whose author today would surely be submitted to the care of a psychiatrist and classed as urgently in need of psychotherapy, tended to awaken in the Renaissance rather reactions of fascination and admiration:

On all sides, madness fascinates Man.[33]

But it was not just painters or court "fools" who strayed into the realms of madness but also ordinary people displaying deviant behaviour or apparent mental confusion who received, in these centuries, a toleration and even respect that seems questionable to us today:

In the Middle Ages and the Renaissance the mad were permitted to exist in the very midst of society. So-called "village idiots" [...] were invariably fed and sustained by the other inhabitants of the village.[34]

All this changed radically, however, in the 17th century. Foucault cites as the key date here the year 1656, which saw the founding in Paris, by the royal decree of Louis XIV, of the institution of the Hôpital Général. This institution was the first to be royally empowered to gather together, largely indiscriminately, the mad, the poor and the indigent of a great city in specially designated places of confinement. In the decades just before and after, however, several other similar institutions were founded elsewhere in Paris and in several other cities and regions of France. Interestingly, as Foucault notes, the buildings and precincts used for this new purpose were very often those which had been used, before the dying-out of leprosy in Europe, as "leper colonies" or habitations set aside for the leprous:

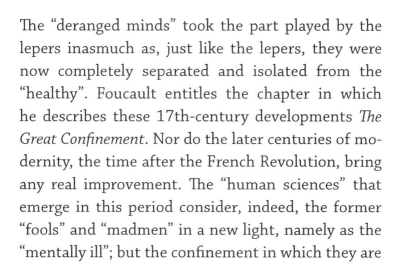

Leprosy disappeared. The leper vanished, or almost, from memory. The structures, (however), remained. Often, in these same places, the formulas of exclusion would be repeated, strangely similar two or three centuries later. Poor vagabonds, criminals and "deranged minds" would take the part played by the lepers [...].[35]

The "deranged minds" took the part played by the lepers inasmuch as, just like the lepers, they were now completely separated and isolated from the "healthy". Foucault entitles the chapter in which he describes these 17th-century developments *The Great Confinement*. Nor do the later centuries of modernity, the time after the French Revolution, bring any real improvement. The "human sciences" that emerge in this period consider, indeed, the former "fools" and "madmen" in a new light, namely as the "mentally ill"; but the confinement in which they are held does not change. The only difference is that the psychiatrists into whose hands these people are now given over no longer wish just to lock them away forever but want rather to heal them and make them fit once again to take their places on the labour market. Thus, the French doctor Pinel, a typical "man of the Enlightenment", became, in 1793 in the midst of the French Revolution, one of the first to declare that madness was not a fate or a destiny but something that could be cured.

But this new therapeutic approach, promising though it sounded, meant in practice, so Foucault argues, no real "humanization" of the treatment of the insane but was rather just a continuation of the old repression in a new form. The "madman", as we have seen, was now redefined, scientifically, as someone "suffering from mental illness", whose "reason" needed to be restored to him. Psychiatrists like Pinel made use, for the first time, of such instruments as strait jackets in order to "pacify" their patients, or regimes of cold showers or specially designed beds and couches in order to stimulate blood-circulation in the brain and bring this latter organ's supposedly reduced functions back again to a normal level. In addition to all this, however, psychiatry, as a newly-invented science, also had a second, much graver consequence:

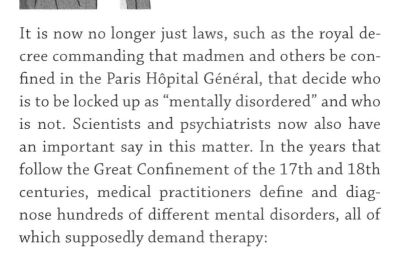

An important phenomenon, this invention of a site of constraint where morality castigates by means of administrative enforcement [...] The law of nations will

no longer countenance the disorder of hearts [...] But in this Great Confinement [...] the essential and the new element is that it is no longer the law that condemns.[36]

It is now no longer just laws, such as the royal decree commanding that madmen and others be confined in the Paris Hôpital Général, that decide who is to be locked up as "mentally disordered" and who is not. Scientists and psychiatrists now also have an important say in this matter. In the years that follow the Great Confinement of the 17th and 18th centuries, medical practitioners define and diagnose hundreds of different mental disorders, all of which supposedly demand therapy:

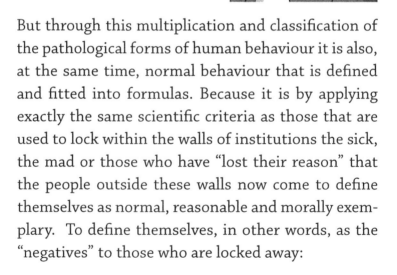

No more than twelve years needed to pass before the three or four categories into which the mentally ill had hitherto been divided

("alienation", feeble-mindedness, violence and mania) proved insufficient to cover the whole domain of madness. The forms of this latter began to multiply [...].[37]

But through this multiplication and classification of the pathological forms of human behaviour it is also, at the same time, normal behaviour that is defined and fitted into formulas. Because it is by applying exactly the same scientific criteria as those that are used to lock within the walls of institutions the sick, the mad or those who have "lost their reason" that the people outside these walls now come to define themselves as normal, reasonable and morally exemplary. To define themselves, in other words, as the "negatives" to those who are locked away:

The walls of confinement actually enclose the negative of that moral city where right reigns only by virtue of a force without appeal [...] and where the only recompense of virtue is to escape punishment.[38]

There exists, Foucault argues, a tremendous compulsion in today's societies to submit and to subjugate oneself to the ruling moral community. This compulsion is early on internalized and is passed on by parents to their children. There predominates, in other words, in our "carceral" society a constant subliminal compulsion to conformity and "normality". "Be reasonable!" is by no means just a well-meaning plea one often hears directed by parents at their growing children; it has been, for several centuries already, the all-overriding imperative of our entire Western civilization. But precisely this, in Foucault's view, represents a deeply unhealthy tendency in the development of this civilization because, however well-organized a culture may be, it always needs madness as a kind of living adversary. It is a testimony, then, to a fundamental weakness and poverty of our own culture that, since around the end of the 18th century, madness has been allowed a voice only in literary form, in the works of a small number of poets and playwrights:

Since the end of the 18th century the life of unreason no longer manifests itself except in the lightning flash of works such as those of Hoelderlin, of Nerval, of Nietzsche or of Artaud [...], resisting by their own strength (our) gigantic moral imprisonment.[39]

Foucault might also have mentioned here certain playwrights of "the theatre of the Absurd", such as Samuel Beckett or Eugene Ionesco, who succeeded, on the stage, in restoring its rights if not to the unreason of madness then at least to nonsense. In terms of the modern age's general tendency, however, the last two or three hundred years have seen a complete exclusion of madness from normal society and a growing determination to deny its existence by never even speaking of it. Today, the powers in control in the world's various states tolerate only a very few forms of "madness", specifically those designed to sustain the state itself, such as the ritual revering of fetish-like symbols like the crossed pieces of wood forming the crucifix. As regards all other forms of madness, it is drilled into us already at school that they are irrational and unscientific.

To sum up, then: in the course of the centuries separating the Middle Ages from our present day, madness has gradually lost its once-important role as a "partner in dialogue" for reason and rationality. This has meant, Foucault argues, that our modern rationality is unhealthily engaged in what can only be described as a monologue, a dictatorial soliloquy in which it relates to itself and itself alone. This modern rationality tolerates no deviation from its own self-dictated principles and creates thereby, in all our modern societies, a universal compulsion to normality.

Discipline and Punish –
The Structure of Our Societies

It is this compulsion to normality that forms the central theme also of what is probably the best-known and most-read of Foucault's works: *Discipline and Punish*, first published in 1975. In this work too Foucault proceeds as an "archaeologist", digging out old documentary sources and chronicles of centuries past so as to shed light on the structure of the practices and institutions of punishment, tracing these through from their earliest forms up to the forms that we observe in the courts and prisons of our present day.

The opening pages of this 1975 book have already attained legendary status within philosophical literature. They present, without commentary and in precise detail, the description, as it had appeared in the year 1757 in the Amsterdam Gazette and in a report by an attending police officer, of the elaborate putting-to-death, culminating in a so-called "quartering", of Robert-François Damiens, who had attempted to assassinate King Louis XV. Foucault begins by reproducing the instructions contained in the sentence itself:

(He is to be conveyed to the) Place de la Grève where […] the flesh will be torn from his breast, arms, thighs and calves with red-hot pincers; his right hand, holding the knife with which he committed the said parricide,

burnt with sulphur; and, on those places where the flesh will be torn away, poured boiling oil and burning resin […]He then moves on to the police officer's eye-witness report of the execution of this sentence:

Though a strong, sturdy fellow, the executioner found it so difficult to tear away the pieces of flesh that he set about the same spot two

or three times, twisting the pincers as he did so, and what he took away formed at each part a wound about the size of a six-pound crown piece […] Despite all this pain Damiens raised his head from time to time and looked at himself boldly

[…] Several confessors went up to him and spoke to him at length; he willingly kissed the crucifix that

was held out to him; he opened his lips and repeated "Pardon, Lord". The horses tugged hard, each pulling straight on a limb […] This

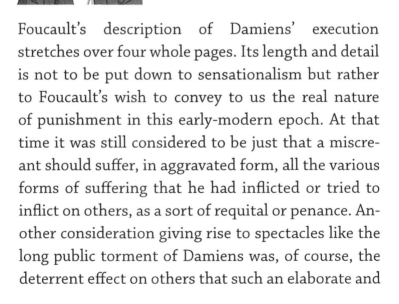

was repeated several times without success [...] The flesh had to be cut almost to the bone; the horses, pulling hard, carried off the right arm first and the other afterwards. When the four limbs had been pulled away,

the confessors came to speak to him but his executioner told them that he was dead, though the truth was that I saw the man

move [...] One of the executioners even said, shortly afterward, that when they had lifted the trunk to throw it on the stake, he was still alive [...].[40]

Foucault's description of Damiens' execution stretches over four whole pages. Its length and detail is not to be put down to sensationalism but rather to Foucault's wish to convey to us the real nature of punishment in this early-modern epoch. At that time it was still considered to be just that a miscreant should suffer, in aggravated form, all the various forms of suffering that he had inflicted or tried to inflict on others, as a sort of requital or penance. Another consideration giving rise to spectacles like the long public torment of Damiens was, of course, the deterrent effect on others that such an elaborate and gruesome martyrdom was likely to have. The Middle Ages and the early modern era offer thousands of examples of such ingenious and elaborate techniques of execution, including "quartering", "breaking on the wheel" and burning at the stake, as well as the more familiar methods of beheading, hanging and drowning. Less grave offences than Damiens', such as theft and other petty crimes, were punished by branding or whipping. In every case, however, the punishment was applied directly to the body.

This changed radically at the beginning of the 19th century. At this period there began to be erected huge prisons in which miscreants could be confined *en masse*. From this point on, violence tends to be inflicted no longer directly on the body but rather on the human consciousness. In this so-called "Age of Enlightenment" the cruel systems of torture exemplified in punishments like that suffered by Damiens became increasingly repulsive to the average citizen and even the criminal came to be recognized as, after all, a human being. The principle also began to be recognized that, if someone was imprisoned, the length of his sentence should not be left up to the arbitrary will of a king or other ruler but should rather be fixed in terms of uniform public laws. These rationalizations of the legal and penal systems, however, and the new efficiency in the passing and execution of sentence, had as a consequence an explosion in the number of convicts, resulting in turn in the construction of many new prisons, often of entirely new types.

The prototype of the new, modern-style prison that emerged in the early years of modernity was provided by the philosopher of law and architect Jeremy Bentham. In 1830 he sketched out a model for a "panoptic prison" which had the advantage of requiring only a very small number of warders. This was achieved by arranging the cells in such a way that the few warders were provided with a view that was "panoptic", a word derived from classical Greek meaning "all-seeing":

> The Panopticon is a building in the shape of a ring in the middle of which there is a courtyard with a tower at its centre. The ring is divided into a series of small cells [...] and in the central tower sits a warder [...] Consequently, everything that the individuals in the cells do is exposed to the gaze of the warders [...] while the warder himself remains unseen.[41]

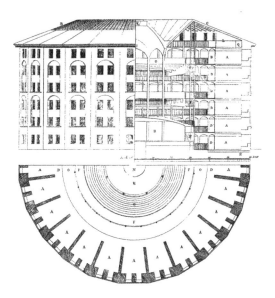

The effect of this arrangement is that the convicts feel themselves to be observed even when the warder is not in his tower:

[…] The inmate must never know whether he is being looked at at any one moment; but he must be sure that he may always be so.[42]

In this way, the inmates behave off their own bat as if they are constantly under surveillance; one might even say that they maintain surveillance on themselves:

> He who is subjected to a field of visibility, and who knows it, assumes responsibility for the constraints of power; he makes them play spontaneously upon himself; he inscribes in himself the power relation in which he simultaneously plays both roles; he becomes the principle of his own subjection.[43]

Such a development, of course, spares the state both time and money and it is still a welcome one even for the penal system today. The goal, however, is no longer today, as it was in Bentham's time, simply that of efficiently confining and supervising the offenders but rather their moral improvement and reintegration into the labour market. Recent years have seen attempts by a whole range of psychiatrists working in forensic disciplines to diagnose, in experts' reports, and to provide suggestions for therapy for, crimes believed to have their roots in one or another form of mental illness. Psychologists closely follow the progress of prison inmates during their sentences and document their "good behaviour", that is to say, its normalization to conform with the accepted standards of society. On their release, social workers and probation officers continue this work. This more professionalized and medicalized treatment of criminal offenders typical of the penal system of the last century is usually celebrated as a more "humane" and "progressive" way of dealing with crime and punishment. But Foucault is concerned to draw attention to aspects of such procedures that are not captured by this narrative of humanity and progress. With the rise of the "human sciences" criminality ceased, indeed, to be demonized as "the work of Satan" and became, for the first time, defined in both legal and scientific terms as a loss of norm-directed self-discipline under the influence of strong emotion, or as a deliberate disregarding of society's norms and laws. But this reconceptualization of criminality in scientific terms proved very soon to give rise to new forms of coercion and compulsion of its own, indeed to coercions and compulsions in many ways more rigid and rigorous than those that existed in the days of torture and of mere crude incarceration. Power is still exerted but now it is exerted, instead of by individual kings or other autocrats, by a great army of scientists, judges, doctors and social workers. They define what is normal and what is abnormal and thereby impose a supposedly "humanely" legitimated compulsion to conform to the model of normality:

The judges of normality are present everywhere. We are in the society of the teacher-judge, the doctor-judge, the educator-judge, the social-worker-judge. It is on them that the universal reign of the normative is based and each individual [...] subjects to it his body, his behaviour, his gestures, his aptitudes, his achievements.[44]

The great theatre of public torment and "quarterings", such as Robert-François Damiens', has, in our modern societies, been replaced by a thousand smaller theatres which all go to sustain the compulsion to "normality":

This, then, is how one must imagine the punitive city [...] Hundreds of tiny theatres of punishment.[45]

Already in Bentham's writings we find the suggestion that panoptic designs and structures might be applied not only in prisons but also, for example, in schools, factories, army barracks or hospitals, with a view to making all the processes performed in these institutions completely transparent. Foucault shows how these suggestions of Bentham's have actually been taken up and how these new, modern techniques of surveillance and supervision are being applied, for example, in schools. Bells signalling the beginning and end of activities, enforcement of punctuality and of uniform dress and posture, a "panoptic" visibility of all in their rows of desks and benches, rhythmically scheduled recesses, physical exercise and permanent checking on "good behaviour" are all practices taken over, ultimately, from the penitentiary model:

And in this ensemble of compulsory alignments each pupil, according to his age, his performance, his behaviour, occupies sometimes one rank, sometimes another.[46]

The "top of the class", the average students, and the "dunces" are all defined in terms of this shifting order of ranks. By means of exams, marks accorded, and even such measures as forcing a student to "do a year over again" the life of school students is constantly hierarchized, structured by punishments and rewards, and organized in terms of a "panoptic" system of compulsions. In the schools of the 16th and 17th centuries none of these structures were yet in existence. At this period, the teacher usually taught a jumbled group of pupils of all sorts of different ages and degrees of scholarly aptitude, all gathered together into a single schoolroom:

A pupil working for a few minutes with the master, while the rest of the heterogeneous group remained idle and unattended.[47]

But with the transposition of the structure of the penitentiary into the school there occurs a thorough panoptic reorganization of this latter as a "serial space", with the coercive marshalling of the students into units defined by rooms or hallways or according to criteria of age or performance:

The organization of a serial space [...] made the educational space function like a learning machine, but also as a machine for supervising, hierarchizing, rewarding.[48]

In the end, the machinery of surveillance takes hold of the whole of society. Firms begin to record, in their personnel files, all the occasions on which their employees have been absent from work, or have received reprimands or commendations from their superiors. Enormous bureaucratic authorities observe, gather data on, and evaluate millions of individuals with regard to their honesty in paying taxes, places of residence, periods of drawing pensions or unemployment benefits. For this reason, it may be said that the forms in which power is exercised have changed radically since the Middle Ages:

(Power) tends to the non-corporal.[49]

We no longer see kings being driven in golden coaches, visible for miles around, through their domains, forcing subjects to their knees and punishing one or another now and then by way of setting an example. What the modern "disciplinary society" creates is rather an invisible, permanent subjugation to power that the individual imposes on him- or herself:

We are [...] in the panoptic machine, invested by its effects of power, which we bring to ourselves, since we are part of its mechanism.[50]

Instead of being under the sway of a king or other ruler, from whom, at one time, all power proceeded, we are, today, ourselves "part of the mechanism" and "bring its power to ourselves". For this reason, Foucault also sometimes speaks of a "microphysics of power". We need, he argues, in order to understand our present age, an entirely new conception of what "power" is:

Power [...] with its self-creation [...] does not consist in a powerfulness of some few powerful individuals.[51]

In Foucault's philosophy it is no longer, as it had been for example in the Marxist theory of society, clearly identifiable ruling classes and exploiters who keep the machinery of power in operation. Instead, it is networks of institutions, formations of scientific ideas, discourses and individuals that, as "parts of the mechanism", themselves incarnate the production of truth and the associated relations of power:

> Power is not something that is acquired [...] or allowed to slip away. Power is exercised from innumerable points, in the interplay of non-egalitarian and mobile relations.[52]

For this reason, not even the building-up of that society of coercion and disciplinary correction that our modern society has become can be said to have been the consequence of a policy pursued by some powerful elite. On the contrary, this society of coercion has been a consequence of the rise of humanism and the sciences. The telling point, in the end, of Foucault's *Discipline and Punish* is that the supposedly humane penal system, with its novel "panoptic" penitentiary, has become the basis of our entire modern society. Visible physical force, indeed, has been, in recent centuries, less and less applied. Today, in most states, it is forbidden to beat children at school, agricultural workers in the field, and even prisoners in penal institutions. But the place of this receding physical violence has been taken by a psychological violence which is in fact much more encompassing. The systems we have described of uniformization, surveillance and coerced self-subjugation have by now become ubiquitous. The behaviour of every citizen of a modern state is influenced and moulded by these systems, whether he is aware of it or not. Everywhere, in workplace, subway or supermarket, each one of us knows what is expected of him. Where, previously, control was exerted over us by kings and other rulers, the subjugation to society's norms is now something performed by ourselves on ourselves.

To sum up, then: conditions like those of the prison, in Foucault's view, are now to be found in all areas of our experience. The modern penitentiary has become the model for society as a whole, so that this society now operates as a persistent and universal coercion to normality, although, since we are now so thoroughly coerced that we have ourselves become "part of the mechanism" of power, our subjugation to the norms of society is a self-subjugation. We are no longer, indeed, whipped or subjected to other forms of corporal punishment. But there is to be found almost universally in the modern subject a certain inward yielding to the constant constraint to be "normal". Modern Man, we may say, is the governor of his own prison, which is himself.

The "Dispositive" of Sexuality

The concept "dispositive", which is often translated in the English-language versions of Foucault's books as "device" or "apparatus", is one of Foucault's key ideas, perhaps **the** key idea of his entire philosophy. What does this word mean? It is composed of the two words of Latin origin "positive", meaning "posed" or "recognizable", and "dis-", a prefix which indicates something that is at odds with whatever the former word states to be "recognizable".

The word "positive" is often used colloquially as a synonym for "good", in the sense for example of "good news" or a "good experience". In its scientific usage, however, it bears the simple Latin sense we have just mentioned: "recognizable". For example, the sentence "the test of the patient's blood for the pathogen proved positive" might be rephrased as "a pathogen was recognized to be present in the patient's blood". As we have also said, however, the prefix "dis-" expresses an exclusion or deviation, something at odds with what is "recognized". As in the words "dis-harmony", "dis-crepancy" or "dis-tantiation", "dispositive" expresses a non-agreement or non-coincidence with what is "recognized to be" the case. In other words, the concept contains both the dimension of "recognition" and the dimension of "segregation" of whatever does not fit this "recognized state". It is surely for these reasons that Foucault makes such frequent use of the word and notion.

In the French military "dispositive" is defined as follows: "a set of deployment methods which are 'disposed' according to a fixed plan".[53] Distinction is made between offensive dispositives and defensive dispositives. An offensive dispositive, for example, would be the fixed plan for a coordinated deployment of infantry, artillery, tanks and aeroplanes. Such an offensive dispositive "recognizes" what is to be done in such an attacking deployment and how and where it is to be done. The prefix "dis-", however, describes what is excluded, what is to be omitted or, in short, all that which must at no price be done during such an attack. For example, no unit should press so far forward on its own that it loses all linkage to, and thus all support from, other units. An offensive dispositive, then, can be said to "qualify" what is to be done and to "disqualify" whatever it is that is never to be done.

Foucault too initially uses the term "dispositive" entirely in this military sense of a strategically coordinated set of deployment methods applied to achieve a specific end. In Foucault's sociological use of the notion, however, the end that is aimed at is not just the guiding of one single attack or retreat but rather that of society as a whole. The "dispositive", as a set of methods deployed, prescribes, in Foucault's usage of it, what society as a whole is to do or refrain from doing:

What I am attempting to grasp with the concept [dispositive] is [...] a set of things decidedly heterogenous in nature comprising discourses, institutions, architectural installations, regulating decisions, laws, administrative measures, scientific pronouncements, philosophical, moral or philanthropic doctrines – in short, a multitude of things both spoken and unspoken.[54]

Thus, for example, the "dispositive" which we have examined above, comprising practices of incarceration and the general compulsion to normalization which arose from these practices, can be said to have been a result of a combination of Bentham's new style of prison architecture, modern judicial institutions, new texts of laws, the administrative registration of all criminal offenders and indeed of all citizens, and finally of the new philanthropic idea, emerging in the Enlightenment, that the aim of justice should no longer be to torture or "quarter" criminals but rather to improve and re-socialize them:

So much for the elements of the dispositive. The dispositive itself is the network that can be woven between these elements.[55]

The "dispositive", then, in Foucault's work, is the entirety of all those decisions taken before our birth or full adulthood within which our lives unfold. It is the network, or in other words the common denominator or quintessence, which guides us, restricts us and prescribes for us the limits of this self-unfolding.

And since each respective dispositive, in this sense, represents something which decides and determines in such a powerful and extensive way all that we say, think and do, Foucault considers the most important task of philosophy to be that of "archaeologically" disinterring dispositives and recognizing them for what they are. This, indeed, is a complicated matter. The dispositive generating that "compulsion to be normal" which we have examined above, for example, was one which was established through the action of a whole set of new sciences and institutions and comprises, as Foucault says, "a multitude of things both spoken and unspoken".

The American sociologist Erving Goffman has explained this composition of the Foucauldean "dispositive" out of "things both spoken and unspoken" very clearly, using the example of the "true American male": "[...] In an important sense there is only one complete, unblushing male in America: a young, married, white, urban, northern, heterosexual Protestant father of college education, fully employed, of good complexion, weight and height, and a recent record in sports [...] Any male who fails to qualify in any of these ways is likely to view himself, during moments at least, as unworthy, incomplete and inferior."[56]

These remarks of Goffmann's cannot, indeed, be said to describe the actual process of emergence of a "dispositive" productive of "good Americans" but they certainly describe the massive effects of this dispositive. Goffman here, then, confirms Foucault's approach in at least one important respect. The network and interconnected set of demands that bring into being the "good American" consists, indeed, on the one hand in "things spoken". The demand that the "true American male" be married, for example, means a dependence on what is "spoken out" by the law of the land and in the institutions that implement it, such as the registry of marriages, births and deaths. It also, however, clearly also consists in "things unspoken", such as the expectation that this male be "fully employed, young and with a recent record in sports". These latter things are nowhere "spoken out" in laws written or publicly pronounced but they everywhere exert a subtle influence and effect. Like an invisible directing hand, they prescribe for every individual the course his or her life is going to take:

What I am attempting to grasp with the concept [dispositive] is [...]

a set of things decidedly heterogenous in nature comprising [...] things both spoken and unspoken.[57]

In his four-volume work *The History of Sexuality*[58] Foucault works out, using a wide range of sources, the "dispositive of sexuality". He shows how this dispositive has changed in the course of time from antiquity up to the present day, that is to say, how each epoch has been characterized by different images and forms of what we believe it is, and means, to "live out one's sexuality". How have human beings, in all these different epochs, used their sexuality to define what they were? In certain epochs, for example, there existed a powerful "knowledge-formation" which created in the people of the day a sense and understanding of themselves as unchaste, vicious, sinful and repentant for their sins; in other epochs, by contrast, a correspondent "knowledge-formation" demanded of people that they define themselves as beings driven by urges and instincts who should, if they were to be healthy, live out their sexual urges in particular to the full and confess to therapists any aspect of their sexuality that they had failed to live out, with the therapist then treating this failure as something to be "cured".

Foucault's assumption is that the various different epochs' different ways of handling sexuality can tell us a great deal about the definition of "the human" in each respective epoch. He raises the question of the "dispositive of sexuality", i.e. the question of what "spoken and unspoken" norms we subject our desires, pleasures and sexual inclinations to in present-day society. What kind of surveillance do we exercise over ourselves? What official and institutional definitions of permitted and forbidden sexuality do we live by and how have they developed up to this point in history?

Foucault develops his concept of a "sexual dispositive" already in the first, introductory volume of the *History of Sexuality: The Will to Knowledge*. Up until now, he argues here, the history of sexuality has in fact been completely wrongly understood, since it has been built up around what Foucault calls the "repressive hypothesis". According to this hypothesis, sexuality was subject, throughout most of the modern era – most famously in the notoriously "straight-laced" Victorian age – to strict repression. This repression, however, so the "hypothesis" continues, began to be lifted in the following century, that 20th century that has produced our own world, first with the "talking about sex" that set in with Sigmund Freud and soon led to the "Sexual Revolution" of the 1960s. All this the "repressive hypothesis" holds to be a process of "liberation" and the "lifting of taboos". Foucault's key argument in his own history of sexuality, however, is this is, in fact, to set things completely on their head. Far from "talking about sex" and all that followed from it's having been brought us freedom, the veritable **command** to talk about one's sexuality that began with Freudianism, and the immediately ensuing overflowing tide of scientific investigation and definition of different types of sexual fulfilment and the techniques to attain them have given rise precisely to a modern "dispositive of sexuality", through which we now find ourselves enslaved:

[...] Our civilization possesses no *ars erotica*. In return it is undoubtedly the only civilization to practice a *scientia sexualis*.[59]

Whereas, for example, ancient Indian culture had possessed, with its Kama Sutra, an "erotic art" which inspired the imagination, our modern Western civilization practices the scientific analysis and classification of sexuality by "sexologists". Sexual pleasure was divided up into "healthy", "sick", "deviant" and "perverse" forms which had to be subjected to more or less elaborate therapy the farther they deviated from the norm. In addition to sodomy, Foucault relates, both onanism and homosexuality came, in modern Europe, to be classified as "pathological" and were thus discredited, and made subject to certain legal sanctions, compulsory therapies and other measures. The female sex in general, he goes on, came to be subjected to certain labels and classifications, even to certain pathological stigmatizations, such as that "women naturally tend to be nervous and hysterical".

Towards the end of the 19th century there was established a powerful dispositive guiding and coercing toward a certain "healthy heterosexual sex-life" which tolerated no deviations. And not just that. Also part of our modern "dispositive of sexuality" is an actual compelling of people to speak about any sexual deviations, or any formative infantile sexual experiences, that they may have undergone, with a view to discovering and exposing their "innermost self" and, where necessary, proceeding to the "curing" of this "innermost self" through therapy. This "inner self" and "inner life" becomes the object of research and investigation for a veritable army of psychiatrists, psychoanalysts and psychologists:

Ours is, after all, the only civilization in which officials are paid to listen to all and sundry impart the secrets of their sex.[60]

But this internalized compulsion to confess one's sexual desires and one's intimate life does not begin just with Sigmund Freud's recommendation that everyone expose their erotic biographies and their repressed wishes but rather starts already in the Christian Middle Ages. Foucault speaks of a lengthy history of "confession culture". Psychotherapists, today, are simply continuing the same practices as were engaged in by priests in their confessionals and repeating the demand made by these priests on those who confessed to them, namely, that they produce the "truth" about their pleasures:

Since the Middle Ages at least, Western societies have established the confession as one of the main rituals we rely on for the production of truth: the

codification of the sacrament of penance by the Lateran Council of 1215, with the resulting development of confessional techniques [...].[61]

The "confession", indeed, as Foucault points out, has been extended nowadays, in contradistinction to the Middle Ages, to all areas of life and society:

The confession has spread its effects far and wide. It plays a part in justice, medicine, education, family relationships and love relations, in the most ordinary

affairs of everyday life and in the most solemn rites; one confesses one's crimes, one's sins, one's thoughts and desires, one's illnesses and troubles [...].[62]

77

This process of general and universal confession began in the Christian Middle Ages and is now, in modern Europe, reaching a terrible consummation:

Western Man has become a confessing animal.[63]

This culture of confession, argues Foucault, is deeply harmful because it facilitates the exercise of power on a massive scale. It brings about an intense and comprehensive surveillance of human beings' inner lives, this being the case both in private love-relations and as regards the public sphere:

The most defenceless tenderness and the bloodiest of powers have a similar need of confession.[64]

The combination of this "confession culture" and of the new "sciences of sexuality" makes possible, in particular, a deeper and deeper penetration of political power into the most intimate spheres of human experience. Foucault here coins a new term: "biopolitics". In our modern societies we see how it is becoming mandatory to confess and register various forms of illness and to undergo vaccinations and other preventative measures, all in the name of ensuring "public health".

In short, then: all of the three large monographs that Foucault published have, in fact, a common thematic core. *The History of Madness* is centred on the dispositive which compels to a distinction and separation of reason and madness, "normal" and "abnormal"; *Discipline and Punish* is centred on a dispositive of confinement which is aimed at separating the "delinquent" from the "decent" but which at the same time serves to define both groups and keep both in check; and in *The History of Sexuality*, finally, he tries to shed light on the dispositive of sexuality itself, which condemns deviations, compels to confessions, and guides and governs sexuality both in the private and the political realms.

In all three studies, then, Foucault is concerned to reveal the systems of compulsion and coercion in which our daily lives play out.

Foucault's core idea is easily recognizable, then: our thinking, speaking and acting are never free; all of these things unfold only within the rigid frameworks of the ruling "discursive truths". For Foucault, there is no discourse at all that can rightly be described with the phrase coined by a famous philosophical contemporary of his: "domination-free discourse" (Habermas). Rather, each and every discourse is guided and governed, as if by invisible hands, by the dispositives that lie behind it. These dispositives do not, indeed, determine in precise detail what we say or do in any particular moment; but they do determine the latitude that we have to speak, act or even think in, and the limits of this latitude.

Human discourse and discussion, then, never really discovers or generates truths of its own but is rather always the mere agent of the dispositives that lie behind and beneath it. The philosopher, then, has the task of bringing to light, much as an archaeologist or an archaeological historian would, the history of the emergence of those dispositives which currently govern and order our world. It is logical then, that the work which first establishes Foucault's characteristic theory and method should be called *The Order of Things*:

It is not a matter of establishing what kinds of powers are weighing upon science from outside it but rather of finding out what sort of power-effects

are circulating within scientific statements themselves [...] It was just these different power-systems that I attempted to describe in *The Order of Things*.[65]

The Order of Things and the Disappearance of Man

It was with the publication of *The Order of Things* in 1966 that Foucault ascended into the "Olympus" of major philosophers. Although certain passages of this book operate on a very abstract level it is, surprisingly, a work that has found many readers outside of the specialized areas it deals with. It sold over 30,000 copies in its first months on the market and came quickly to replace the works of Sartre as the book passed hand to hand and passionately debated in the cafés of the Left Bank. The magazine *Le Nouvel*

Observateur ran the headline: "Foucault Selling Like Hotcakes". And indeed one of the great cultural-political events of these mid-1960s in France was the way Foucault suddenly spectacularly toppled the famous Existentialist from his throne as "philosophical king of Paris". This and his other writings were soon translated and received worldwide recognition. Foucault was fully aware of the role that he now came to play:

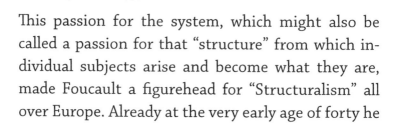

We experienced the generation of Sartre as a generation that was, indeed, courageous and generous, a generation with a passion for life, politics, existence. But we ourselves discovered something else, a different passion: a passion for the 'system', if I may call it so.[66]

This passion for the system, which might also be called a passion for that "structure" from which individual subjects arise and become what they are, made Foucault a figurehead for "Structuralism" all over Europe. Already at the very early age of forty he was appointed as a professor at the eminent Collège de France, a chair being created especially for him and his structure-based research project with the title "History of Systems of Thought".

"Structuralism", indeed, had not been created by Foucault but rather, some decades earlier, by the Swiss linguist Ferdinand de Saussure with his provocative thesis to the effect that language is not, as it is generally held to be, a product of speaking human beings but rather these human beings themselves products of language. It is, argued Saussure, only within the structure of language that we can express and develop our subjectivities; Man, then, is a product of his own systems of signs.

The logician Wittgenstein might also be said to have been arguing as a "Structuralist" when he wrote that: "The limits of my language mean the limits of my world".[67] According to a basic contention common to both Saussure and Wittgenstein, we are incapable of ever saying or even thinking anything outside of the structure of our language, since these things are both inconceivable except in the form of words and propositions. It is a contention that can be tested by anyone at any time. One need only try to formulate or express a thought without using words or some form of sentence in order to discover that it is indeed impossible. This suffices to prove structural linguistics' claim that language determines our understanding of the world and sets the limits to this understanding.

Some years later, Claude Lévi-Strauss transposed this radical approach into his own field of anthropology, showing in his four-volume work *Mythologiques* that it is not really human beings who can be said to actively and freely invent their myths; rather, he argued, myths tend to have such a powerful effect on human beings that they are, in the last analysis, more real and more basic than individual humans themselves. Myths leave their mark on our self-understanding. It is, in a sense, not human beings that create stories but stories that create human beings. Proceeding very consistently here, Lévi-Strauss applies this notion of being surrendered up completely to narrative structures even to himself and the way he personally feels: "I appear to myself as the place where something is going on, but there is no 'I', no 'me'. Each of us is a crossroads where things happen. The crossroads is purely passive. Things happen there. A different thing, equally valid, happens elsewhere. There is no choice [...]"[68]

Foucault too, initially, subscribes to this radically Structuralist notion of the vanishing of the self and the total passivity of the individual. In *The Order of Things* he describes how the world was cognitively organized and ordered in various different epochs and how individuals alive at these epochs had to comply with this ordering. Each era has, he argues, a different way of seeing things and therefore a different understanding of the meaning of life. Thus, the "order(ing) of things" peculiar to each epoch creates not just a form of self-understanding for the people living in it but also a range of institutions, constitutions, rules, rituals, economic and legal structures and indeed the structure of reality as a whole. The individual human being is a product of this structure or system, not its producer. Today, Foucault is usually classified as a "post-Structuralist" but, for a very long time, he too shared the Structuralist "passion for the system" that we have heard him talk about:

That which passes profoundly right through us, that which is there before us, that which sustains us in time and space, (is) the *system*.[69]

It was only a late turn toward a critical reflection on the topics of dispositives and an active "art of living" that catapulted Foucault out of the class of the pure Structuralists and made him a "post-Structuralist". In the 1966 *Order of Things*, however, he still takes a strictly Structuralist approach, dividing the whole modern history of the West and its inhabitants into three great systems of cognitive ordering: the Renaissance of the 16th century, the "Classic Age" of the 17th and 18th, and the properly speaking Modern era, beginning around the time of the French Revolution at the very end of the 18th. Each of these three periods has its own cognitive system or structure or, as Foucault phrases it, its own *épistèmè*. This Classical Greek word means, essentially, just "knowledge". But Foucault gives to it a special philosophical twist and depth, using it to refer to the specific cultural form or framework that underlies and gives shape to all the different forms of "knowledge" and "science" that enjoy resonance and validity in a specific epoch:

In any given culture and at any given moment there is always only one

épistèmè that defines the conditions of possibility of all knowledge.[70]

The *épistèmè* of the Renaissance, Foucault argues, or in other words the underlying form moulding all this epoch's knowledge, is "representation", or i.e. similarity or analogy. That is to say, there were sought, against the background of the cosmological world-picture of the "Great Chain of Being", similarities and analogies between things traceable back to their common origin in the hands of the Creator. Thus, for example, the Renaissance mind was fond of discovering similarities between the body of Man and the structures of the planet he lives on:

His flesh is a glebe, his bones are rocks, his veins great rivers, his bladder is the sea [...].[71]

Despite this, however, the earthly existence of Man continued to be understood in this epoch, as it had been in the preceding Middle Ages, in terms of Man's sinfulness and in expectation of a grace of God that would be endowed on him only in the world beyond. A radical change here comes about only in the following two centuries, the 17th and 18th, an epoch which the French often designate as "the Classic Age" and which is often referred to, indeed, outside France, using the name of the long-reigning French king of the period, as "the Age of Louis XIV". This was also the Age of Enlightenment which saw the birth of many of the "human sciences" and thus involved a radical re-ordering of the way the world was perceived and classed. The new *épistèmè* of this epoch demanded now, instead of mere analogies, a concordance of all the things in the world with certain words and names:

The fundamental task of Classical "discourse" is to ascribe a name to things and in that name to name their being.[72]

The "Classic Age", then, loves synopses, labellings, and systems of classification. This Classical *épistèmè*, however, is soon succeeded by another: from the 19th century onward the new *épistèmè* prescribes that knowledge about the world and all that is in it must be scientifically checkable, that is to say, in conformity with the truths established by the various types of science and scientists. In other words, the human being is turned into an "object": an object specifically of such sciences as biology, psychology, economics or human genetics.

For a biologist like Darwin, for example, Man is no longer a creature of God but rather just a higher type of mammal. For a psychologist like Freud he is a being driven by instinct, for an economist like Marx one driven by material need whose very thoughts are defined by the "mode of production" he lives in. The scientific truths on which these claims are based, however, are in all three of these cases truths made by Man himself. Timeless, metaphysical, "indefinable" truths such as "God's justice", "honour" or other "noble virtues" become less and less important and relevant.

Foucault believes that the radical changes occurring in human experience between the epoch of knowledge based on "analogy" and "resemblance" and that of knowledge based on "scientific truth" can be clearly seen by the example of the hero of Cervantes's novel *Don Quixote*. The tragedy of *Don Quixote*, so runs Foucault's argument, is that he continues, in the midst of the new capitalist world, to defend the noble knightly values which form an *épistèmè* which, in his lifetime, has long since been superseded:

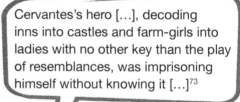

Cervantes's hero [...], decoding inns into castles and farm-girls into ladies with no other key than the play of resemblances, was imprisoning himself without knowing it [...][73]

Don Quixote, in other words, imprisoned himself, without knowing it, in a world that no longer existed. He clung stubbornly to the mode of "truth-production" characteristic of the Middle Ages and thus became, from the perspective of the newly-arisen modern *épistèmè*, a madman and an object of mockery. Foucault thus not only drastically demonstrates to us how the new scientific mode of perception and organization radically overthrew the old "order of things"; he arrives, in the end, at a highly provocative prognosis:

[...] Man (is) erased, like a face drawn in sand at the edge of the sea.[74]

By this he does not mean that our species will die out, for example through some such disaster as climate change, but rather simply that Man as a self-determined subject would cease to be:

[...] The end of Man [...] is just a particular case, or if you wish a particularly visible form, of a much more general 'dying-out'. I mean

by it [...] the death of the subject, of the "subject with a capital 'S', the subject as origin and foundation of knowledge, freedom, language and history.[75]

It is Man as "subject with a capital 'S'", then, Man as origin and foundation of knowledge, freedom, and language, that is in the process of dying out. The reason for this is simple. In the 19th century Man made himself the object of his own scientific research and thereby gradually disempowered himself. The main "human sciences" emerging in the modern period, which were psychology, economics, biology and linguistics, began, indeed, by trying to prove through research that Man was a free, conscious subject; but as these researches progressed they began all to point to the conclusion that Man is totally bound in, in all he does, to pre-existing structures:

> When investigation began of Man as a possible object of knowledge [...] what one ended up encountering was a certain 'unconscious', an unconscious shot through with drives and instincts [...] which had absolutely nothing to do with that essence of Man, or human freedom, that one had hoped and expected to find.[76]

Biology too, just like psychoanalysis, produced in the end a set of very disappointing and sobering results. Instead of being able to locate some organic basis for the much-praised "free spirit of Man", biology was able to discover only later after layer of genetic pre-programming, from hair-colour to intelligence quotient:

In biology [...] the chromosomal chain bears, in coded form, all the information that is necessary for the development of each individual living being.[77]

The same applies to linguistics:

People had hoped that, by studying [...] the evolution of various grammars and comparing languages with one

another, there would reveal itself some sort of "essence of Man" [...] But what did one actually find by digging about in language? One found structures.[78]

Once his modern *épistèmè* had developed to full maturity, then, Man found himself to be determined by forces he could not control. He found himself slowly sinking into the quicksand of biologically pre-coded processes, of mechanisms of unconscious regulation, of macro-economic necessities of the market, ending up imprisoned within systems of language and concepts which existed before him. In other words, he abolished himself as a self-determined being:

The present day proves beyond doubt that Man is on the point of vanishing.[79]

But this "death of Man" that Foucault predicts is not so regrettable as it might at first appear. Because this "Man" who is about to die away is, after all, only the self-determined rational "Man" of the human sciences who was invented as recently as the 19th century. He is that type of "Man" who believes that he can know, categorize and discipline all the things of the world and has thereby brought upon this world all kinds of misery. And one should not forget, adds

Foucault, that this human type who is characterized by this drive to research and classify himself even to the point of abolishing himself is, in the last analysis, only one of the many possible types of knowing human being that history has brought forth in the course of time:

As the archaeology of our thought easily shows, Man is an invention of recent date.[80]

And when this "Man" who is the "Man" specifically of our modern "disciplinary society" vanishes, his place may well be taken by some new and better form of knowing subject articulated with some new and better organizing *épistèmè*.

Of What Use is Foucault's Discovery for Us Today?

Foucault's Panopticon Prison: The Prototype for Digital Surveillance?

Of what use is Foucault to us today? Is he right in claiming that we all find ourselves in a "disciplinary society"? Are we, like the prisoners described by Bentham, permanently under observation, so that we tailor our behaviour to the knowledge that we are always observed? Are we really each of us "our own prison governors"?

If one stops and considers for a while the core idea of Foucault's philosophy one cannot help but notice that it is a philosophy which calls into question everything that has always generally counted as "progress" and "progressive": for example, the empathetic therapeutic treatment of mentally ill people by psychiatrists, psychologists, psychoanalysts and associated institutions, or the replacement of capital and corporal punishment by more humane ways of handling criminals. For Foucault, indeed, neither of these sets of reforms represent any true progress:

[...] And "reform" in the strict sense [...] was a strategy with the primary objective of making of the punishment

and repression of illegalities a regular function, co-extensive with society [...] to punish with an attenuated severity, perhaps, but only in order to punish with more universality and necessity.[81]

It is hard not to concur at least with the latter part of the thesis advanced by Foucault here. Punishment is inflicted in the present day with less severity perhaps but greater universality. That is to say, such gruesome individual spectacles as the "quartering" described above have now been replaced by a universal, supposedly "preventative" mass surveillance of entire populations. The exercise of power and violence, in other words, has nowadays dispensed with its former "spectacular" trappings but continues, nonetheless, to exert a cruel and powerful discipline in a more subtle way:

> [...] The perfection of power tend(s) to render its actual exercise unnecessary.[82]

Is Foucault right here? Are we really at the mercy of an increasingly subtle power-mechanism the exertion of whose power-effects can barely be perceived by us any longer? Certainly, it is the case that, today, we find ourselves, without our being really aware of it, institutionally registered, surveilled, and administered from our first breath through to our last, via birth certificates, compulsory schooling, mandatory vaccinations, drivers licences, employment and unemployment benefit regulations etc. In some countries, it is even mandatory to inform the authorities each time one changes address. But Foucault's suspicion that we may have entered a universal surveillance society becomes an even more urgently relevant one if one takes into account the new possibilities offered by digital technology. Foucault himself had known little of these. During his lifetime there existed no more sophisticated devices than video cameras mounted in shops or on street corners to ensure against shoplifting or motorists breaking the speed limit.

He would most likely turn in his grave if he saw the technologies of surveillance in use today. Entire metropolises can now be kept under constant video surveillance. Biometric data are gathered as a matter of course. Facial recognition software makes it very easy to locate anyone anywhere at any time. The traces we leave online make it possible for companies to create detailed consumer profiles for each individual on the planet. And exactly as Foucault had predicted, we have become, just like Bentham's prisoners in the "Panopticon", accustomed to and accepting of this condition of being constantly seen and observed. With every credit-card purchase, every Google search, and every post on an online forum, we make the system still stronger:

We are [...] in the panoptic machine, invested by its effects of power, which we bring to ourselves, since we are part of its mechanism.[83]

This "panoptic machine" is now more and more being used by states and governments with a view to disciplining populations. China, for example, has notoriously introduced a "social credit" system which, on the basis of close and constant surveillance, awards citizens positive and negative points depending on how "exemplary" or how "deviant" their observed behaviour has been.

A Chinese citizen, for example, who is picked up by face-recognizing surveillance equipment crossing a road against a red light or throwing a paper cup onto the street instead of a dustbin will find that points have been deducted from his or her centrally-databased "social credit account". But besides these unambiguous, even if trivial, offences, many other actions of a much more ambiguous and arguably innocent nature, such as delays in paying bills, looking at pornography on the Internet, or critical remarks made about the party or the government, all tend to go to affect such citizens' "credit scores". Whoever ends up, after all this, with less than 1000 points is classed as a "bad person" and the citizens so stigmatized then find themselves under pressure to raise their "score" once again by displaying especially compliant and exemplary social behaviour, so as to recover the esteem of their fellow citizens:

He who is subjected to a field of visibility, and who knows it, assumes responsibility for the constraints of power; he makes them play spontaneously upon himself; he inscribes in himself the power relation in which he simultaneously plays both roles; he becomes the principle of his own subjection.[84]

Many Chinese today, in fact, approve of such a system as a fine way to encourage all citizens to perform good deeds. The "social credit" system was first fully introduced in 2014 in the coastal city of Rongcheng, whose approximately 670,000 inhabitants were asked to regularly present, whenever they were seeking a promotion at work or a loan from the bank, a statement of the points on their "social credit account". Another early pilot project for all-inclusive data-gathering on every aspect of Chinese citizens' lives was a programme called "Honest Shanghai". By now the "credit score" system has been implemented almost everywhere in China. Whoever sinks, for example due to financial irregularities, below a certain point-level finds he or she can no longer buy a ticket for a train or plane. Already in 2018 this punishment was imposed, according to official Chinese court statistics, some 6.7 million times.[85] But also in the West "panoptic" systems are being introduced. Both in the US and in many European countries policemen now wear body-cameras which record all their interactions with the public. This measure might be said to encourage both sides in such interactions to moderate their behaviour and it appears to have led to fewer assaults on police. But Foucault would certainly have seen in such projects a further triumph of the "panoptic machine":

> The seamlessly continuous system of punishment [...] which gathers and checks data at every moment [...] produces a standardizing, uniformizing, normalizing effect.[86]

One can retort to Foucault's scepticism here that this coercive normalization does indeed tend to have the positive effect of seeing to it that fewer crimes are committed in the first place. Thus, for example, Bill

Gates, the great Internet pioneer, pointed up already thirty years ago this possibility of digital crime-prevention. In his book *The Road Ahead* he envisages a future in which the location and the movements of every human being on the planet could be tracked, for example, by a chip implanted in a tooth which would be constantly sending signals to a satellite, much as a GPS locates and tracks millions of cars. The "diary" of each person's movements could, initially, remain sealed and confidential but with a sufficient number of satellites enough data could be gathered and maintained for the police to be able to know, in principle, in every single case of a criminal offence just who was at the scene of the crime at the relevant time; something that would surely lead to a massive reduction in criminal activity.

Gates concedes that certain citizens may be concerned about data protection here and not wish to be constantly tracked. But the automatically recorded "movement diaries" would, for just this reason, initially be sealed and confidential, so that the citizen charged with a crime would have to allow the prosecutor or judge access to this "diary": "Your wallet PC will be able to keep audio, time, location, and eventually even video records of everything that happens to you. It will be able to record every word you say and every word said to you, as well as body temperature, blood pressure, barometric pressure, and a variety of other data about you and your surroundings. We can think of the wallet PC as an alibi machine, because encrypted digital signatures will guarantee an unforgeable alibi against false accusations. If someone ever accused you of something, you could retort: 'Hey, buddy, I have a documented life. These bits are stored away. I can play back anything I've ever said. So don't play games with me'."[87]

Gates also points to the small country of Monaco in which, since video surveillance has been introduced in all streets, shops, underpasses and public transport, "criminality has practically died out".[88] But whereas Gates points out here the opportunities afforded us by digital data-gathering Foucault warns us against the dangers of any such panoptic surveillance. He even points out what, theoretically, such a development could eventually lead to:

The perfect disciplinary apparatus would make it possible for a single gaze to see everything constantly.[89]

The Invisible Hand Behind Everything: Recognize the Dispositive!

Foucault once described, in an interview, his books as "toolboxes":

All my books [...] if you wish, are little toolboxes. If people want to open them and make use of some phrase, idea or analysis as if it were a screwdriver [...] in order to short-circuit, delegitimate or otherwise shatter systems of power, then all the better![90]

And one can indeed work with certain of Foucault's concepts as if with workman's tools, even if it does not always prove possible to "short-circuit power systems" with them. The most dazzlingly multi-layered concept in Foucault's "toolbox" is surely the "dispositive". The dispositive lies, like an invisible hand, behind all coercions and compulsion, be they visible or merely felt. It is the epicentre of all our lives' limiting specifications and draws its force from a whole network of institutions, traditions and knowledge-formations:

The dispositive itself is the network that can be woven between these elements.[91]

One can interpret Foucault's proposal that his books be used as "toolboxes" as an encouragement to engage in the following exercise: find dispositives!

Let us take one example. Anyone who makes the mistake of taking some books of Foucault's on holiday with him will inevitably find himself asking, after a few days: "what is the dispositive of the 'good holiday-maker'?" A holiday is, in fact, not the completely uncoerced and unconditioned thing that we like to imagine it is. On closer examination, we can see that it is subject to a whole series of imperatives. One is positively under an obligation, when on holiday, to "relax", to be "spontaneous", to "live in the moment". And whenever one feels that one has achieved these goals there appears to be an equally binding obligation to record one's achievements by means of "selfies" and so on.

The structures indispensable for meeting these specifications, which are nowhere written down but nonetheless implicitly present, are created by the holiday-maker already when he books his holiday. Firstly, some location far from his daily working existence: another region or country or the famous "desert island". Secondly, access to the sea. Thirdly, some accommodation in which the noise of planes carrying other arriving and departing holiday-makers is not too audible. Fourthly, acceptable conditions in terms of weather, food, rest and leisure activities which facilitate the prescribed "relaxation".

In short, then: above all when "on holiday", I am in fact in the grip of a whole series of demands and structures for which I pay and to which I am obliged to conform if I am to succeed in making myself into what others and indeed my own self demand of me: a "good holiday-maker". To this end I hand myself over, consciously and deliberately, into the grip of powerful touristic systems equipped with vast capacities for transport so that these systems can constitute me as a "relaxed holiday-maker". But what sort of dispositive lies behind all this? A friend once provided me with a hint regarding the actual truth of the matter here. He has himself, for many years, to the great annoyance of his partner, refused to go on any sort of holiday at all. He justifies this by saying: "my life as a musician is very important to me; I have no need of 'taking a break' from it; on the contrary, I'm afraid of anything that might distract me from it." And indeed, unlike for this friend of mine, holidays are for most of us attempts to distract ourselves for a little while from that working life in which we feel ourselves to be cut off largely or even wholly from our real needs and desires. Is, then, the sought-after "holiday dispositive" a flight from a condition of distress, or a response to it?

I understand by "dispositive" a kind of, let us say, formation the principal function of which has consisted, at any given point in history, in responding to an urgent critical situation. The dispositive, therefore, has a primarily strategic function.[92]

And indeed, the introduction into our societies of the "holiday dispositive" was, as Foucault supposes is the case for all dispositives, a strategic response to a social situation of distress. It was, for example, in Germany before the First World War, such factors as the terrible overworking of many employees, who often put in a twelve-hour day, and the fear of an ever-growing number of voters for the Social Democratic Party, perceived as a possible source of a Communist revolution, that led to the introduction of the first legally-prescribed holiday entitlements. That is to say, if there was set up at this time a dispositive of the "good holiday-maker" and a kind of "duty to relax" introduced across an entire society, this was done only in order to stabilize and protect the still more important dispositive of "the good worker". Still today provisions exist in German employment law specifying that no activities contrary to the requirements of rest and recreation should be demanded of the employee during holidays.

In short, then, the dispositive of the "good holiday-maker" is to be understood, from Foucault's point of view, as a strategic response to the urgent critical situation of widespread alienation in normal working life. That life which was not truly lived during working days and weeks must, for strategic reasons, be compensated for by a time-limited "liveliness" during holiday periods, so as to preserve the socially more imperative dispositive of a society based on work, effort and "results". If one sometimes has the odd feeling, then, that one is being "forced to relax" during holidays and vacations, this is not an illusion but rather ensues from the real social need to take measures to deal with the "unlived life" that all of us suffer from. It also raises the question of whether it would not be healthier to try rather to find ways to "live more" in the normal course of daily working existence.

The concept of the dispositive, therefore, opens up for us many possible ways of explaining situations which one may have vaguely felt to be constraining or oppressive. For example, at least well into the 20th century it was common for mothers to do their best to make their children swallow, every day, a spoonful of cod liver oil. The unpleasant memories, nursed by members of certain generations, of the foul taste of this concoction sting less, perhaps, if there is borne in mind the Foucauldean truth that the mothers in question did not do this out of wickedness but rather on the basis of a sense of moral obligation to comply with the "health dispositive" of the day. This dispositive prescribed that the only way to ensure the healthy development of a child was to dose him with such "tested medical remedies" as cod liver oil.

It was a prescription typical of an era of blind faith in "medicine", when doctors were still revered as "gods in white coats". But once such a dispositive has been established, it tends to create its own milieu, as Foucault makes clear to us by the example of the dispositive of incarceration:

Let us take as an example incarceration: that dispositive which brought it about that, at a certain point in time, such measures as arrest and imprisonment appeared to be the most reasonable

and effective ways of dealing with the phenomenon of criminality. What effect was produced by this? One which absolutely could not have been foreseen or predicted: the constitution of a whole "milieu" of delinquency.[93]

Through the mass incarceration of "delinquents" and the separation of these latter from the "normal citizens" two irreconcilable milieus, the "criminal" and the "normal", were brought into being. From this point on, the non-incarcerated began to define themselves as the morally good, by virtue of their obedience to the norms. And just like this dispositive of incarceration, so too did the dispositive of health which we have just referred to create – at least in people's minds – two separate social milieus: the parents who supposedly understood how to properly nourish their children and the parents who supposedly did not, the former group being those who regularly dosed out the foul-tasting cod liver oil. To use Foucault's "toolbox" to recognize larger and smaller dispositives does not, of course, necessarily mean to remove these dispositives. But it can perhaps mean beginning to think about alternatives to them:

Philosophy is a movement with the aid of which [...] one can free oneself from that which generally counts as "true" and go in search of other rules by which one might live.[94]

If We Are Part of the Structure of Discourse, How Are We to Break Out?

Foucault describes and analyses in a very trenchant way the subtle discourses and systems of coercion which set the tone for our lives together in society and tell us what is healthy and what is sick, what is normal and what is perverse, what is morally decent and what is criminal, as well as what can be allowed to freely develop and what must be "re-socialized", be it through therapy or through punishment and incarceration. But there remains in the end the great question of just what Foucault is trying to tell us with his analysis of power and discourse. Is he merely trying to describe these systems of coercion or is his concern to change and reform them from the bottom up? And if the latter, then how does he envisage our going about this? Can we really succeed in abolishing, and replacing with something better, these institutions and sciences which, according to Foucault himself, gave rise to the exclusions, the surveillance and the coercion that we still experience today but whose history goes right back to the 17th and 18th centuries?

Foucault gives no answer to this question. It is indeed impossible for him to do so. Because by doing so he

113

would contradict his own most basic idea. Foucault emphasizes again and again that every discourse is an expression of power and of the dispositives corresponding to this power. There can be, then, no real "break-out" out of whichever discursive logic happens at any given time to predominate, since we ourselves as subjects, along with all the beliefs we hold, arise always only out of the prevailing discursive reality:

> Discourse is the entirety of coerced or coercing meanings which pass through and inform all social relations.[95]

For this reason, there can be so such thing, on Foucault's terms, as a "critique of ideology" in the sense in which this notion was developed by Marxists and by some of his contemporaries, such as Habermas, who have partially relied on Marxist insights: namely, that of a critique exposing how views and opinions are manipulated and revealing the manipulating interests behind this. In terms of Foucault's philosophy it simply makes no sense to investigate what an individual says or thinks from the point of view of how far it is "manipulated" and how far it corresponds to actual truth. No clear line of separation, argues Foucault, can ever be drawn between "manipulation" and "scientific truth", since science itself often follows "untrue" knowledge-formations:

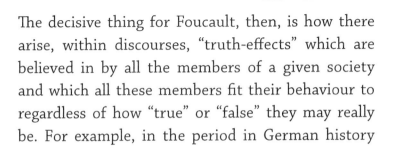

It is just that, in my view, the problem does not consist in drawing distinctions, within a discourse, between that part of it which may depend upon truth and that part of it which may depend on

something other than truth. Rather, it is a matter of looking, historically, at how "truth-effects" emerge within discourses which are, just in themselves, neither "true" nor "false".[96]

The decisive thing for Foucault, then, is how there arise, within discourses, "truth-effects" which are believed in by all the members of a given society and which all these members fit their behaviour to regardless of how "true" or "false" they may really be. For example, in the period in German history

115

when such concepts as "the health of the Volk", "purity of blood" and "racial struggle" came to dominate speech in public and private contexts, the decisive thing was not so much all that was actually false in such language as the question of how such a fatal "knowledge-formation", and thus the reality which its acceptance created, could have arisen. And one of the things that Foucault points out, indeed, is how the relatively new scientific disciplines of biology and evolutionary theory, with their scientific claims regarding mutation and selection and indeed the Darwinian "survival of the fittest", had, even though such disciplines are generally looked on as part of the movement of "Enlightenment", largely contributed to these dark regressive developments:

The "Enlightenment", which discovered the liberties, also invented the disciplines.[97]

Foucault demonstrates again and again how those ideas which are generally accepted by us as "truths" and are treated in the prevailing discourses of our modern world as examples of sure and certain "scientific knowledge" were in fact specifically "produced" as such at various points in human history. Such "disciplines" as biology, psychology, economics and other sciences, along with the institutions that they inform and that support them, in fact "produce" all the things that pass, within them and within the wider society, for "truth" and "knowledge". Thus in German National Socialism, for example, it was certainly not just the single central figure of the "Fuehrer" who single-handedly produced and proclaimed all this cruel society's false "truths". This work was in fact also done by a large number of less prominent institutions, such as the many professorial chairs and seminars in "racial theory" which were turning out, in this period, massive amounts of supposedly "sure and certain knowledge" about racial evolution and selection. The power of such "truth-production" proceeded not from one source but from a "machinery" consisting of many sources:

[...] Power [...] functions like a piece of machinery [...] It produces fields of objects and rituals of truth. The individual and his knowledge are results of this production.[98]

Even we ourselves today are, as individuals, along with all we take to be our "knowledge", products of just such "truth-production" and "rituals of truth". There is, then, ultimately no way out for us from the constraining structures of these discourses. Every opinion, however "personal" it may seem, is thoroughly pervaded by the respectively predominant "power-knowledge" constellation and its dispositives and, in the last analysis, a product of the structure:

[…] One is "in truth" only when one obeys rules set by a certain invisible discursive "police" which one is obliged to reactivate in every one of one's speech-acts.[99]

We must, then, honestly recognize that all that we are inclined to look on as "our own opinions" really arises from a network of pre-existing institutions, traditions and truth-producing sciences. For this reason, argues Foucault, attempts to improve society simply by appealing to "humanistic" values will always fail and prove pointless. "Humanism", indeed, as a form of knowledge arising in the course of Enlightenment, has itself played a fatal role in the emergence of a "disciplinary society". Even plainly coercive systems like Marxism and Communism, with their ideals of total equality, can be traced back to "humanist" discourse.

But of what use, then, are Foucault's analyses if everything, in the end, is just a question of power and we ourselves, as individual subjects, are inevitably lost and dissolved in the objective structures? One critic of his work has said of Foucault that, although he has "rattled the bars of the iron cage" that he believes even our modern enlightened society to be, he has not "developed any plan or project for turning this cage into something that might look like a home."[100] And we do indeed not find in Foucault's work any proposals for social reforms. But he has contributed something important just by his descriptions alone. He has shown us that the "truths" conveyed by all our currently predominant discourses and by the dispositives that underlie them are not given by Nature but have rather come into being historically. Which means that they can also change or pass away with history. However bound into the dispositive we may be, we receive from the mere information that it arose historically a certain encouragement to test out other ways of thinking and perceiving. And just this is the true task of philosophy:

Philosophy consists in that shifting of the framework of thought, along with all the other forms of work that must be performed, if one is to think differently, act differently and be differently from how one currently is.[101]

We can, then, despite our being so firmly bound into the structures of truth-production of our respective epoch, think otherwise, and become otherwise than we are. With this claim Foucault gives a last unexpected twist to his philosophy. As a young man, he began his philosophical career by disinterring, as an "archaeologist", those rigid structures that leave their mark on our lives and indeed constitute these latter. In his later work, however, he begins to encourage us to study these apparently immovable structures with a view, after all, to putting them into question and thus freeing ourselves to some extent, at least in our minds, from their control. Some commentators have viewed this as an inconsistency on Foucault's part. But it is perhaps just this inconsistency, just this final paradoxical twist that Foucault gives to his own philosophy, that also gives to his thought that moment of inner tension to which it owes its worldwide fame and success. Instead of holding stubbornly to Structuralism, he encourages us, especially in his later work, to recognize the limitations of all he had taught before and to push on, partly, outside these limits.

Foucault's Legacy: Making One's Own Life a Work of Art

This turn away from purely Structuralist thinking, or its widening to include new perspectives and a new emancipatory philosophy, is a move that Foucault performs above all in the second and third volumes of his multi-volume *History of Sexuality*: the volumes with the titles *The Use of Pleasure* and *The Care of the Self*. Both these volumes appeared almost simultaneously, in 1984. Foucault had read their final proofs in his bed in the Salpêtrière hospital in Paris, where he died later that year, at the young age of 57, from the then-incurable HIV virus.

What was radically new in these final works was Foucault's engagement with the ethics of ancient Greece and Rome and specifically these cultures' art of living: the "care of the self".

In contrast to his earlier works he here no longer investigates just the historical developments and structures which continue to mark our modernity but gives us insight also into certain long since abandoned historical practices concerning how to deal with one's own subjectivity. He describes the moral notions and ethical behaviour of the Greeks and Romans from the 4th century BC up until the 1st and 2nd centuries AD.

Using Latin and Greek texts written by Plato, Epicurus, Rufus of Ephesus, Musonius, Seneca, Plutarch, Epictetus, Marcus Aurelius and others, Foucault investigated in these volumes the ethical discipline and moral behaviour prescribed in the Classical era of Greece and in that period of the Roman Empire which still stood under the influence of Hellenism. The results he arrives at are astonishing. He finds in all the authors he examines, unanimously, a set of ethical prescriptions which do not demand that behaviour be oriented to laws or prohibitions but rather urge that individuals practice a "care of the self". Foucault, for example, refers to the Stoic Epictetus:

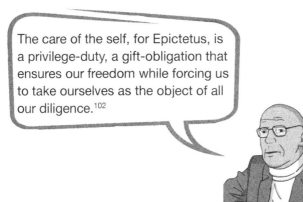

The care of the self, for Epictetus, is a privilege-duty, a gift-obligation that ensures our freedom while forcing us to take ourselves as the object of all our diligence.[102]

Seneca too, argues Foucault, advances the same view, especially emphasizing the practice of proper life-conduct. Seneca advocates devoting all the resources of one's freedom, one's whole life long, to "creating oneself", "transforming oneself":

Seneca [...] asked people to transform their existence into a kind of permanent exercise.[103]

Just like Epictetus and Seneca, even that Classical writer who is generally looked on as a "hedonist", Epicurus, placed "the care of the self" in the centre

123

of his philosophy. Although Epicurus looked on the "pleasure principle", i.e. the avoidance of pain and the pursuit of pleasure, as the best guide for living a good life, we find even in his writings an exhortation to deal with desires in a measured and moderate way and to pursue also a higher training of the soul. This, he says, applies especially to young people:

> [...] The Epicureans [...] began by stating (that) it is never too early or too late to care for the wellbeing of the soul.[104]

Foucault comes finally, in these last of the studies he published, to the following conclusion:

> [...] Each of us needs to cultivate this "care of the self". Greek and Graeco-Roman ethics were centred on the problem of personal decision: the problem of an aesthetics of existence.[105]

"Aesthetics" means "the doctrine of the beautiful". With the phrase "aesthetics of existence", then, Foucault is surely trying to express the idea that the people of Classical Greece and Rome looked on their lives as "total artworks", so to speak, on which they wished to endow both an inner and an outer beauty. The Greeks and the Romans had, indeed, just like us certain moral ideas about how to live their lives, the propriety of their sexual practices and the right way to deal with physical pleasure. But these ideas, argued Foucault, were not defined, as they tend to be today, in terms of rigid laws, biblical commandments, or moral codices:

The principle according to which this activity was meant to be regulated [...] was not defined by a universal legislation determining permitted and forbidden acts but rather by a *savoir-faire*, an art [...].[106]

Instead of on laws and prohibitions the ancient Greeks relied rather on an "art of moderation". They practiced an "aesthetic of existence":

What I mean by this is a way of life whose moral value did not depend [...] on one's being in conformity with a code of behaviour [...] Through [...] the relation to truth that governed it, such a

life was committed to the maintenance of an [...] order (and also) took on the brilliance of a beauty that was revealed to those able to behold it.[107]

The Greeks, then, were concerned with free and self-responsible action with regard to the truth and beauty of their own lives. In fact, "the use of pleasure" was much less regulated in ancient Greece than it is today. Neither homosexual love between men or between women nor even paedophilic love between grown men and young boys was subject to any legal restriction. It was simply left up to the responsibility, and sense of moderation, of each individual citizen not to do harm to others by allowing his or her desire for pleasure to get out of control. The same principle, in other words, applied in business, in politics, and in respect of one's own sexual self-expression. Although everyone was assumed to possess a basic ability to moderate their own desires in this way, Epictetus reports certain exercises for strengthening this ability:

There were certain exercises through which self-mastery could be acquired. The point, according to Epictetus, was to be able to look at a beautiful girl or boy without feeling desire. But to do this one must be completely master of oneself.[108]

Ascetic practices too, then, were also very important for the "art of life" in ancient Greece and Rome. The Greek word askesis, however, did not just mean "continence" but also, and primarily, "exercise". These exercises included the acquisition of virtues, the consolidation of character, healthy nourishment and the philosophical exercise of the mind. Because it is only that individual who has learned to moderate "the use of pleasure" and of his needs that is truly master of himself and able to give form to his life:

> [...] The will to be a moral subject and the search for an ethics of existence consisted, in the ancient world, above all in the effort to affirm one's own freedom and to give a certain form to one's life.[109]

The affirmation of the freedom to seek a form for one's own life was something that later, with the arrival of Christianity, was lost. In its place there were set up strict commandments. From now on, people were no longer to decide themselves what was good and bad, beautiful and ugly, morally exemplary or reprehensible. Rather, they were expected to follow the rules and rituals of the Church:

> With the transition from the Classical world to Christianity one passed from a morality which was essentially the search for a personal ethics to a morality which consisted just in obedience to a system of rules.[110]

Still today people often take their bearings, in moral questions, by codices passed down through the religious tradition:

[...] That one has no right to have sexual intercourse with anyone except one's wedded wife: that is, for example, an element of the codex.[111]

Homosexuality too is still, in many countries around the world, a crime. But, even though Foucault was himself homosexual, his concern in these final investigations of sexuality was less this or that particular restriction on his or other's sexual freedom than it was outlining the problem of how people in the ancient world found, or created for themselves, a "self". Since there existed in this distant epoch no prior specifications, or at least far fewer of them, for what action was moral and what was not, the great task consisted in finding one's own style in life:

This working out of one's own life as a personal artwork [...] stood, it seems to me, in the centre of the moral experience, of the "will to morality", in the ancient world.[112]

The Cynic Diogenes proceeded in this way, fashioning his own life into a lived form of radical freedom. He gave up all security, prosperity and family and spent most of the day lying in a tipped-over wine-barrel that served as his only "home". If the stories told about him are to be believed, he once mounted a ladder leant on the wall surrounding the marketplace and recounted to the citizens all that he said he could see on the other side. The things he recounted were, of course, invented but they were so entertaining that the people gave him food and other gifts. Diogenes was an "artist of life". The citizens of Corinth mockingly called him "the Dog" because he slept in a barrel and was always to be found trailing around the marketplace. But Diogenes embraced this insulting nickname. When the famous Macedonian king Alexander came to visit the city during one of his campaigns and greeted him with the words "I am Alexander the Great", he replied "And I am Diogenes the Dog". According to Plutarch, when Alexander asked him what favour he, as most powerful man in the world, could do for him, Diogenes replied: "Get out of my light". It was just so proudly and uncompromisingly as this that Diogenes embraced his "style of life" of freedom without material needs.

To "make one's life an artwork", however, did not mean necessarily to give up all concern with social significance, social responsibility and even the exercise of power. The "soldier-emperor" Marcus Aurelius was a good example of "the care of the self" in the manner of the Stoic philosophers. He gave to his life an inner beauty by exercising the office of emperor in a completely selfless way and leading, during the last ten years of his rule, an ascetic existence in tents set up on the sites of his military campaigns. Many other biographies from this time could be cited, such as that of the tutor Seneca or the slave Epictetus, showing how these individuals developed, through their actions and their attitude, an "aesthetic of existence". They modelled and perfected their own lives like the sculptor models and perfects his statue:

> The individual fulfilled himself as an ethical subject by shaping a precisely measured conduct that was plainly visible to all and deserving to be long remembered.[113]

This special form of "the care of the self" represents, in the last analysis, a moral attitude which is at the same time free and responsible and which slipped gradually, in the following centuries, completely out of the reach of Western mankind:

> What interests me about this idea is a notion contained in it that lies nowadays somewhat distant from us: namely, that the work which we have to perform is not a thing that is separate from us but rather simply our own life, our own self.[114]

With these remarks Foucault was not idealizing the world of the ancient Greeks and Romans. He was fully aware, of course, that the style of life "at the same time free and self-responsible" that he was describing was a style of life reserved for the freeborn male citizens of these societies and refused, for example, to women and to slaves. He also recognized that the ancient "art of living" was not something that could simply be transferred into the present day:

The wheel of time cannot be turned back.[115]

Nevertheless, Foucault's whole purpose in describing in all its facets that ancient Greek and Roman model of an "aesthetic of existence" was to provide us with a closer view of something which, in recent centuries, has slipped out of our reach, indeed has fallen into a kind of disrepute: namely, "the art of living". Today, Foucault points out, we tend to look on the person who "treats his own life as a work of art" as a rather suspicious, disreputable character. Our instinctive feeling is that such a person, if they secure themselves the freedom to develop the creative and artistic aspects of their self, necessarily does so "on the backs of others", with others paying the cost. Such a man, we suspect, avoids or refuses a regular job and completely rejects the dispositive of the "society of real results":

> We're inclined to suspect there's something immoral in what I have called "the care of the self" and that it's just a way of getting out of following the rules that apply to all.[116]

Foucault, however, for his own part, sees in this act of moral and aesthetic self-determination an important opportunity:

> I am fascinated by the idea that an "ethics of existence" can, just in itself, provide a strong structure without having to fall back on a system of law or public authority or a disciplinary structure.[117]

Many, of course, have critiqued and rejected this, Foucault's plea for an "ethics of existence". Some have argued that it is incompatible with the Structuralist approach he had worked with for so long and represented a collapse back into the "philosophy of the individual subject".[118] The philosopher and sociologist Habermas even reproached him with having promoted, with his late work, a selfish and apolitical attitude to life.

But Foucault emphasizes at many points in these late analyses that the Greek and Roman "aesthetic of existence" also requires the recognition of one's actions by others and therefore certainly does possess a political dimension. Foucault's students[119] have pointed out, for example, that Greta Thunberg, with her "school strike" intended to draw attention to climate change, has, in her way, "made an artwork of her life". Her decision, likewise, to travel to the Global Climate Conference in a sailboat so as to avoid CO_2 emissions might be described in terms of an "aesthetic of existence" which sent, nonetheless, a strong political message. "Life as artwork" can, then, very definitely be a political matter.

Nevertheless, Foucault fears that such an idea of "life as art" is being, with very few exceptions, more and more thoroughly eliminated from the modern world.

Nowadays, art is mostly only tolerated in museums, as if in temples:

I am struck above all by the fact that art, in our societies, has become something which concerns only objects, not individuals or individuals' lives.[120]

In museums we look up reverently at the pictures. Experts explain to us their particular aesthetics and the exciting lives led by the artists. We ourselves, however, vanish under the compulsion to normalization in the mediocrity of our existence. But this is not the way it has to be. Foucault encourages us to see through the way that we are bound into the ruling dispositives and power-structures. He urges us to recognize the knowledge-formations of the "disciplinary society" and to put them into question. The compulsion to normalization will surely continue to exist; we see it before our eyes every day. But perhaps it is time to follow the path mapped out by Foucault's vision and to cease to treat this compulsion with respect:

Why should each of us not be able to make an artwork of his or her life?[121]

Bibliographical References

1   Michel Foucault, Discipline and Punish: The Birth of the Prison, Vintage Books, New York, 1977, Second Edition, p. 217.

2   Michel Foucault, Dits et Ecrits 1954-1988, Volume 4, 1980-1988, Gallimard, Paris, 1994, p. 42. (This four-volume collection of Foucault's many interviews, speeches and shorter articles has not yet been fully translated into English. We therefore cite the French editions. The translations are our own.)

3   Ibid. p. 41.

4   Michel Foucault, The Order of Things, Routledge Classics, London and New York, 2002, p. 422

5   Ibid. Vol 1. 1954-1969, p. 818.

6   Michel Foucault, in Von der Subversion des Wissens, Fischer Publishing House, Frankfurt am Main, 1987, p. 87.

7   Michel Foucault, Dits et Ecrits 1954-1988 Volume 1, 1954-1969, Gallimard, Paris, 1994, p. 498.

8   Michel Foucault, Madness and Civilization, Vintage Books edition, New York 1988. The phrase "Great Confinement" is used as the title of the second chapter of this book.

9   Ibid. p. 124.

10 Michel Foucault, Discipline and Punish: The Birth of the Prison, Vintage Books, New York, 1977, Second Edition, p. 202.

11 Ibid. p. 207.

12 Ibid. p. 205.

13 Michel Foucault, Dits et Ecrits 1954-1988 Volume 1, 1954-1969, Gallimard, Paris, 1994, p. 499.

14 Michel Foucault, Dispositive der Macht, Merve Publishers, Berlin, 1978, p. 51.

15 Ibid.

16 Michel Foucault, History of Sexuality, Volume One, The Will to Knowledge, Random House, New York, 1978, p. 11.

17 This major work, planned as comprising five volumes, ended up comprising only three: The Will to Knowledge, The Use of Pleasure, and The Care of the Self. The fifth volume was never written and the fourth, with the title Confessions of the Flesh, was published only in

2018, thirty-five years after Foucault's death. The reason for the delay was that Foucault had strictly forbidden all posthumous publication of his work and his legal heirs, at least initially, strictly respected this wish. And in fact it is noticeable that Confessions of the Flesh was not thoroughly revised by its author. Titles were added afterward and there are many repetitions. Foucault gathers in this book many sources drawn from Christian writers between the 2nd and the 4th centuries writing on the way that sexuality should be handled and dealt with. Missing here, however, is the stringent sociological and philosophical ordering of the material that usually characterizes his works. If a "main thesis" can be made out in this last work at all, it is the thesis that it was through Christianity that the question of dealing with sexuality became, for the first time in history, the core question of human subjectivity. This self-examination of the individual, with regard to an ascetic manner of dealing with the libido supposedly pleasing to God, became a central preoccupation with the rise of Christianity and continues to leave its traces even in our late modernity. For all the virtues of this final, posthumous work, however, scholars still tend to look on the first three volumes of The History of Sexuality, which had enjoyed the benefit of Foucault's own final editing, as the more significant books.

18 Michel Foucault, Dispositive der Macht, Merve Publishers, Berlin, 1978, p. 1.

19 Michel Foucault, Dits et Ecrits 1954-1988 Volume 1, 1954-1969, Gallimard, Paris, 1994, p. 498-9.

20 Ibid. Volume 4, 1980-1988, p. 205.

21 Ibid. Volume 1, 1954-1969, p. 801.

22 Michel Foucault, Die Ordnung des Diskurses, Fischer Publishers, Frankfurt, 1991, p. 25.

23 Ibid. p. 10 ff.

24 Michel Foucault, Autobiographie, in German Magazine for Philosophy, Vol. 42, Issue 4, Akademie Verlag, Berlin, 1994, p. 699 ff.

25 Michel Foucault, Dits et Ecrits 1954-1988 Volume 3, 1975-1979, Gallimard, Paris, 1994, p. 217.

26 Michel Foucault, History of Sexuality, Volume Two: The Use of Pleasure, Random House, New York, 1985, p. 8.

27 Ibid.

28 Michel Foucault, Madness and Civilization, Vintage Books edition,

New York 1988, p. 37.

29 Ibid. p. 121.

30 Michel Foucault, Dits et Ecrits, 1954-1988 Volume 1, 1954-69, Gallimard, Paris, 1994, p. 169.

31 Michel Foucault, Madness and Civilization, Vintage Books edition, New York 1988, p. 121.

32 Ibid. p. 21.

33 Ibid. p. 23.

34 Michel Foucault, Dits et Ecrits 1954-1988 Volume 2, 1970-75, Gallimard, Paris, 1994, p. 133.

35 Michel Foucault, Madness and Civilization, Vintage Books edition, New York 1988, p. 7.

36 Ibid. p. 60 (translation altered).

37 Michel Foucault, Histoire de la Folie à l'Age Classique, Gallimard, Paris, 1972, p. 408.

38 Michel Foucault, Madness and Civilization, Vintage Books edition, New York 1988, p. 61.

39 Ibid. p. 278.

40 Michel Foucault, Discipline and Punish: The Birth of the Prison, Vintage Books, New York, 1977, Second Edition, pp. 4-5.

41 Michel Foucault, Dits et Ecrits 1954-1988 Volume 2, 1970-75, Gallimard, Paris, 1994, p. 594.

42 Michel Foucault, Discipline and Punish: The Birth of the Prison, Vintage Books, New York, 1977, Second Edition, p. 201.

43 Ibid. pp. 202-03.

44 Ibid. p. 304.

45 Ibid. p. 113.

46 Ibid. p. 147.

47 Ibid.

48 Ibid.

49 Ibid. p. 203.

50 Ibid. p. 217.

51 Michel Foucault, History of Sexuality, Volume One, The Will to Knowledge, Random House, New York, 1978, p. 87.

52 Ibid. p. 94.

53 Foucault-Handbuch, edited by Clemens Kammler, Rolf Parr and Ulrich Schneider, Metzler Publishers, Stuttgart 2014, p. 238.

54 Michel Foucault, Dispositive der Macht, Merve Publishers, Berlin,

1978, p. 119 ff.

55 Ibid. p. 120.

56 Erving Goffman, Stigma: Notes on the Management of Spoiled
    Identity, Spectrum Books, New Jersey, 1963,   p. 128

57 Michel Foucault, Dispositive der Macht, Merve Publishers, Berlin,
    1978, p. 119 ff.

58 Michel Foucault, History of Sexuality, Random House, New York

59 Michel Foucault, History of Sexuality, Volume One, The Will to
    Knowledge, Random House, New York, 1978, p. 58.

60 Ibid. p. 7.

61 Ibid. p. 58.

62 Ibid. p. 59.

63 Ibid.

64 Ibid.

65 Michel Foucault, Dispositive der Macht, Merve Publishers, Berlin,
    1978, p. 26.

66 Michel Foucault, Dits et Ecrits, 1954-1988 Volume 1, 1954-69,
    Gallimard, Paris, 1994, p. 514.

67 Ludwig Wittgenstein, Tractatus Logico-Philosophicus, Routledge and
    Kegan Paul, Oxford and New York, 1974, p. 3.

68 Claude Lévi-Strauss, Myth and Meaning, Routledge Classics, London
    and New York, 1978, p. x

69 Michel Foucault, Dits et Ecrits, 1954-1988 Volume 1, 1954-69,
    Gallimard, Paris, 1994, p. 514.

70 Michel Foucault, The Order of Things, Routledge Classics, London and
    New York, 2002, p. 183.

71 Ibid. p. 25

72 Ibid. p. 132

73 Ibid. p. 228.

74 Ibid. p. 422.

75 Michel Foucault, Dits et Ecrits, 1954-1988 Volume 1, 1954-69,
    Gallimard, Paris, 1994, p. 788.

76 Ibid. pp. 663-64.

77 Ibid. p. 514.

78 Ibid. p. 664

79 Michel Foucault, The Order of Things, Routledge Classics, London and
    New York, 2002, p. 421.

80 Ibid. p. 422.

81 Michel Foucault, Discipline and Punish: The Birth of the Prison, Vintage Books, New York, 1977, Second Edition, p. 82.

82 Ibid. p. 201.

83 Ibid. p. 217.

84 Ibid. pp. 202-203

85 This information was conveyed by a German TV news broadcast from 2019.

86 Michel Foucault, Discipline and Punish: The Birth of the Prison, Vintage Books, New York, 1977, Second Edition, p. 295.

87 Bill Gates, The Road Ahead, Viking Press, New York, 1996, p. 303.

88 Ibid. p. 306.

89 Michel Foucault, Discipline and Punish: The Birth of the Prison, Vintage Books, New York, 1977, Second Edition, p. 173.

90 Michel Foucault, Dits et Ecrits, 1954-1988 Volume 2, 1970-75, Gallimard, Paris, 1994, p. 720.

91 Michel Foucault, Dispositive der Macht, Merve Publishers, Berlin, 1978, p. 120.

92 Ibid.

93 Ibid. p. 121.

94 Michel Foucault im Gespraech, Merve Publishers, Berlin, 1982, p. 22.

95 Michel Foucault, Dits et Ecrits, 1954-1988 Volume 3, 1975-1979, Gallimard, Paris, 1994, p. 178.

96 Michel Foucault, Dispositive der Macht, Merve Publishers, Berlin, 1978, p. 34.

97 Michel Foucault, Discipline and Punish: The Birth of the Prison, Vintage Books, New York, 1977, Second Edition, p. 222.

98 Ibid. p. 177.

99 Michel Foucault, Die Ordnung des Diskurses, Fischer, Frankfurt, 1992, p. 25.

100 Michael Walzer in his essay The Politics of Michel Foucault.

101 Michel Foucault im Gespraech, Merve Publishers, Berlin, 1982, p. 22.

102 Michel Foucault, History of Sexuality, Volume Three, The Care of the Self, Random House, New York, 1986, p. 47.

103 Ibid. p. 49.

104 Ibid. p. 46.

105 Michel Foucault im Gespraech, Merve Publishers, Berlin, 1982, p. 78.

106 Michel Foucault, History of Sexuality, Volume Two, The Use of Pleasure, Random House, New York, 1985, p. 91.

107 Ibid. p. 89.

108 Michel Foucault im Gespraech, Merve Publishers, Berlin, 1982, p. 79.

109 Ibid. p. 135.

110 Ibid. p. 136.

111 Ibid. p. 82.

112 Michel Foucault, Eine Aesthetik der Existenz, Suhrkamp, Frankfurt, 2007, p. 282.

113 Michel Foucault, History of Sexuality, Volume Two, The Use of Pleasure, Random House, New York, 1985, p. 91.

114 Michel Foucault, Eine Aesthetik der Existenz, Suhrkamp, Frankfurt, 2007, p. 199.

115 Michel Foucault im Gespraech, Merve Publishers, Berlin, 1982, p. 76.

116 Foucault quoted in Rux Martin et al, Technologien des Selbst, Fischer Publishers, Frankfurt, 1993, p. 31.

117 Michel Foucault im Gespraech, Merve Publishers, Berlin, 1982, p. 78.

118 Henning Ottman, for example, gives, to the chapter on Foucault in his History of Political Thought, the title Death and Resurrection of the Individual, referring to Foucault's surprising turn away from Structuralism back to a concern with the individual subject. "In Words and Things," writes Ottmann, "Foucault buried Man, describing him as a 'face washed away in the sand'. But in his later work, which investigates the traditions of the 'care of the self' in the ancient world, Man and the individual are resurrected." (See Ottman, Geschichte des Politischen Denkens Vol 4 p. 259). Habermas expresses the same idea even more drastically in his philosophical Discourse of Modernity: "(Foucault's) historical erasure of the individual subject ends in a hopeless subjectivism" (p. 324 of German edition).

119 See Wilhelm Schmid, Die Lebenskunst ist Politisch in Philosophie-Magazin, special Foucault edition, Berlin 2019, p. 90.

120 Michel Foucault im Gespraech, Merve Publishers, Berlin, 1982, p. 80.

121 Ibid.

Already published in the same series:

Walther Ziegler
Adorno in 60 Minutes
ISBN 9783750460232

Walther Ziegler
Arendt in 60 Minutes
ISBN 9783752649031

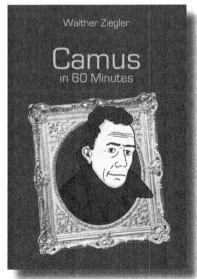

Walther Ziegler
Camus in 60 Minutes
ISBN 9783741227738

Walther Ziegler
Confucius in 60 Minutes
ISBN 9783753423128

Walther Ziegler
Foucault in 60 Minutes
ISBN 978375342688

Walther Ziegler
Freud in 60 Minutes
ISBN 9783741227707

Walther Ziegler
Habermas in 60 Minutes
ISBN 9783752612370

Walther Ziegler
Hegel in 60 Minutes
ISBN 9783741227677

Walther Ziegler
Heidegger in 60 Minutes
ISBN 9783741227752

Walther Ziegler
Hobbes in 60 Minutes
ISBN 9783751968317

Walther Ziegler
Kant in 60 Minutes
ISBN 9783741226373

Walther Ziegler
Marx in 60 Minutes
ISBN 9783741227691

Walther Ziegler
Nietzsche in 60 Minutes
ISBN 9783752803822

Walther Ziegler
Rawls in 60 Minutes
ISBN 9783750424050

Walther Ziegler
Rousseau in 60 Minutes
ISBN 9783741227622

Walther Ziegler
Sartre in 60 Minutes
ISBN 9783741227653

Walther Ziegler
Smith in 60 Minutes
ISBN 9783741227721

Walther Ziegler
Platon in 60 Minutes
ISBN 9783741227615

Walther Ziegler
Popper in 60 Minutes
ISBN 9783750470897

Walther Ziegler
Schopenhauer in 60 Minutes
ISBN 9783750498853

Walther Ziegler
Wittgenstein in 60 Minutes
ISBN 9783750426955

The author:

Dr Walther Ziegler is academically trained in the fields of philosophy, history and political science. As a foreign correspondent, reporter and newsroom coordinator for the German TV station ProSieben he has produced films on every continent. His news reports have won several prizes and awards. He has also authored numerous books in the field of philosophy. His many years of experience as a journalist mean that he is able to present the complex ideas of the great philosophers in a way that is both engaging and very clear. Since 2007 he has also been active as a teacher and trainer of young TV journalists in Munich, holding the post of Academic Director at the Media Academy, a University of Applied Sciences that offers film and TV courses at its base directly on the site of the major European film production company Bavaria Film. After the huge success of the book series "Great thinkers in 60 Minutes", he works as a freelance writer and philosopher.